SHORT COURSE SERIES

# Clockwise

## elementary

## Teacher's Book

Heather Potten &
Jonathan Potten

OXFORD
UNIVERSITY PRESS

# Contents

# Introduction

## Clockwise elementary aims

- to give students varied opportunities to develop greater fluency
- to help students understand spoken English with more confidence
- to cover a range of useful everyday functional language which will allow students to cope in an English-speaking environment
- to present and review essential grammatical areas
- to remind students of useful 'survival' language
- to help students build a wider vocabulary

- to provide ideas which will help students to learn vocabulary more effectively
- to present and practise language in relevant, practical contexts
- to provide students and teachers with varied, challenging material
- to give students a clear sense of personal progress and satisfaction
- to give teachers a flexible course that can be adapted to the needs of their students and the nature of their teaching situation

## Clockwise elementary

### Structure

The Classbook consists of twenty-four self-contained lessons. The focus of these lessons is situational / survival language, the grammar and vocabulary needed to help students communicate, and the four skills: speaking, listening, reading, and writing.

*Clockwise* Elementary has a flexible syllabus, and all the lessons are 'stand-alone'. This means that they are not interdependent – they can be covered in sequence, but they can also be used effectively in any order, depending on students' needs and the nature of the course.

Every lesson follows a similar pattern. There is an opening activity (*Speak for yourself*, *Vocabulary challenge*, *Listening challenge*, or *What do you know?*), followed by the main body of the lesson, which can include vocabulary input, grammar coverage, and situational / survival language. Students practise the language through a variety of activities, and each lesson ends with *Speak out*.

Each lesson is supported by activities in the Practice section at the back of the Classbook, and there is a photocopiable key on *pp.71–79* of this Teacher's Book.

The Teacher's Resource Pack contains photocopiable activities to supplement each lesson. This Pack reinforces the language coverage of the Classbook, and adds a valuable element of variety.

### Timing

Each lesson is designed to last approximately ninety minutes, or longer if the Teacher's Resource Pack and / or Practice section is used too. Actual lesson time depends on a number of factors, such as class size and how involved the students become in the different activities. The Teacher's Book contains comprehensive notes on interaction, timing, classroom management, and methodology, as well as ideas for alternative procedures and extra activities.

### The syllabus

#### Speaking

In *Clockwise* Elementary students learn the language they need to get by in an English-speaking environment, or in situations where they need to communicate in English with speakers of other languages. The emphasis is on providing practical, relevant language, and students cover areas like talking about themselves and their families (lesson 03), discussing likes and dislikes (lesson 07), telephoning (lesson 14), and making travel arrangements (lesson 20).

Ten of the lessons begin with *Speak for yourself*, which builds students' confidence by encouraging them to talk about things that are familiar to them. In this section students often work in pairs or small groups, and there is a wide variety of activity types, including questionnaires, class surveys, and comparing opinions.

All lessons include speaking activities, whether the focus is on grammar, vocabulary, or situational / transactional language. *Useful language* boxes summarize essential language, and provide an easy reference for students to refer back to. Emphasis is placed on students' ability to speak and to understand English, and there is a variety of practice activities. Following practice, students progress to the *Speak out* section, the culmination of each lesson, where they express themselves on a variety of topics using the language covered in that lesson. Activity types include dialogues, discussions, role plays, ranking and ordering, story-telling, and class surveys.

#### Pronunciation

Pronunciation activities focus on the individual sounds of letters, word stress, sentence stress, linking, and intonation. Sometimes the students practise these different skills in isolation. Alternatively they are asked to model their own speech on short listening texts. This provides them with a definite goal, and allows them to concentrate on all the different aspects of pronunciation simultaneously.

#### Listening

The course focuses on short listening activities designed to help students to understand people in a variety of real situations. These range from people talking about themselves, their plans, or their weekend, to a shop assistant discussing items in a shop. The dialogues are intended to help students with the need to understand people talking at native speaker speed. Some are quite challenging, and regular *Teaching tips* offer ideas and suggestions for how to give your students the support they need when doing listening activities.

Each listening is preceded by clear focus questions and tasks, and followed up with a variety of activities such as matching, sentence completion, and form-filling. These activities are short and to the point. There is also 'bottom-up listening', where students focus on the exact words in a dialogue. This kind of decoding can help to build confidence. Sometimes students are asked to refer to the Tapescripts in the back of the Classbook to confirm their answers to activities. This combination of listening and reading allows students to focus on specific language. Full Tapescripts also appear in the teaching notes in this Teacher's Book.

## Grammar

The grammar syllabus covers basic verb forms and tenses, and other areas vital to students' ability to communicate. Each grammar point is presented in a situational context which enables students to understand the reasons behind what they are learning or consolidating. Students are given plenty of chance to practise or revise, before progressing to freer use of the language.

Grammar boxes highlight the form, and, where appropriate, the use, of grammatical structures. These boxes can be referred back to at any point in the book to remind students of key language.

## Vocabulary

A number of lessons concentrate on lexical areas such as countries and nationalities (lesson 02), occupations (lesson 06), opinion adjectives (lesson 10), and food and menus (lesson 16). The aim is to equip students with a range of active vocabulary to enable them to cope with situations they are likely to encounter, both in English-speaking countries and when conversing with other nationalities. Most importantly, activities allow students to apply the vocabulary to their own lives.

There are also regular *Expand your vocabulary* boxes, which give students tips on how to learn vocabulary.

## Reading

*Clockwise* Elementary uses texts from a range of sources to improve students' reading skills. Because elementary students need to be able to cope with difficult texts in real life, some of these texts are only slightly modified from the original, like the city guide extracts in lesson 08 and the film reviews in lesson 10. This encourages students to focus on the main message, and to learn to cope with the presence of unknown vocabulary. Text types include e-mails, biographies, magazine articles, advertisements, and extracts from accommodation guides. Students practise a number of reading skills, including reading for detail, skimming, and scanning.

## Writing

Writing activities appear in both the class material and the Practice material and are of a practical nature, including e-mails, lists, forms, and letters. Students are led from basic sentence patterns to more detailed text construction. Writing is also used to reinforce language learning. Students are encouraged to write short dialogues reviewing work done on speaking, or to write about topics relevant to themselves and their lives.

## Features

### Lesson aims

These are outlined at the beginning of each lesson. They are useful for students both as an indicator of what is to come and to remind them of what they have done.

### Lesson openings

There are four different lesson openings. *Speak for yourself* gets students talking about the topic of the lesson, *Vocabulary challenge* is a quick way of activating relevant vocabulary, *Listening challenge* presents a short listening as a way into the lesson, and *What do you know?* give students a chance to demonstrate their familiarity with the grammar content of the lesson.

###  Against the clock

This is a regular feature of the *Clockwise* series. The idea of using timed activities is to challenge and motivate the students, and to vary the pace of the lesson. The times given are general guides – you may want to give your students more time if they need it, or less time if they are very confident.

### Can you remember ...? boxes

These appear at the end of each lesson to jog students' memories about the content of the lesson. They can also help students prepare for *Speak out*, or be used as revision prompts at any time during the course. The boxes also refer to the Practice section.

### Other margin boxes

The margin contains boxes that give information or tips and highlight relevant language points. There are also reminders of common classroom or process language, like *How do you say _____ in English?* and *What does _____ mean?*

### Interaction patterns

The course contains a number of interaction patterns including individual, pair, group, and class work. The Teacher's Book includes tips on alternative approaches and class dynamics. Information gap pair work activities appear on *pp.105–106* of the Classbook.

## Practice section

There is additional material for every lesson on *pp.76–104* of the Classbook. Features are:

- regular writing practice including form filling, informal letters, e-mails, descriptions, and opinions
- further reading practice
- vocabulary and grammar reinforcement
- regular *Test your spelling* exercises
- review of situational language

The activities can be used in class or for homework, and the key on *pp.71–79* of this Teacher's Book can be photocopied and given to students.

## Lesson aims

- Revise and practise the alphabet.
- Revise and practise dates.
- Focus on useful numbers.
- Give students the opportunity to get to know each other.

## What do you know?

### The alphabet

**The alphabet**
The students will already know the alphabet, but might confuse certain letters, for example the vowels *a*, *e*, and *i*, or the consonants *g* and *j*. Part of this lesson aims to consolidate the alphabet and the students' ability to use it, for example, in spelling their names.

1 Do this as a brainstorming activity. Students can call out their answers to the questions. The vowels and consonants can be written up on the board, in separate sections or in different colours.

### Alternative

Depending on your class, you might prefer to do this as an individual or pair work activity.

1  26
2  5
3  consonants
4  *e* is the most common letter
5  *z* is the least common

2 Focus students on the tip box in the margin. Students can work in pairs or groups to complete the table.

**Feedback:** ask different pairs to present their findings column by column. Check with other pairs that they agree.

**Note**
You may want to introduce your students to phonetic symbols at this stage. The symbols can help students to group the letters by sound. They can also use dictionaries to help if necessary (most dictionaries include a list of phonetic symbols).

| /eɪ/ | /iː/ | /e/ | /aɪ/ | /əʊ/ | /uː/ | /ɑː/ |
|------|------|-----|------|------|------|------|
| a | b | f | i | o | q | r |
| h | c | l | y | | u | |
| j | d | m | | | w | |
| k | e | n | | | | |
| | g | s | | | | |
| | p | x | | | | |
| | t | z | | | | |
| | v | | | | | |

'z' is pronounced /ziː/ in American English

3 This gives students an opportunity to check that they know how to pronounce the letters. Move around the class monitoring their progress, assisting where appropriate.

### Extra

To consolidate students' learning of the alphabet, you could give them a short geographical spelling test. Ask them to spell these words:
Hungary
Japan
Iceland
India
New Zealand

**Feedback:** ask the students to spell back the countries letter for letter.

4 **Against the clock.** Time the class from *a* to see if they can say the alphabet within 20 seconds. Students can continue to the end even if mistakes are made, or you can stop the class at every mistake, asking the next student in line to begin from *a* again. You could repeat this activity as a quick warm-up at the beginning of later lessons.

## Speaking

### Names and spelling

1 This is a mingling activity. Students get up and move around the classroom, completing their own class registers. As they do this, you can move around monitoring for accuracy. Make a note of the letters students are struggling to pronounce in order to revise them later.

2 Students check their work in pairs.

**Feedback:** students can read out their work so that all the names can be written up on the board to check the spelling.

### Alternative

This section of the lesson can be skipped if your class already know each other well. Instead, you could do a spelling dictation. Ask students to write down the names of three famous people. In groups of three or four, students take turns to spell out the names on their lists. The first student to guess the name of the famous person wins a point. This will help consolidate learning of the alphabet.

## English in use

### Dates

1 **Against the clock.** Tell the class that they have just two minutes to write down the names of the months. They do not have to be in order – students should write whatever they remember. Then they can check their work in pairs and put the months in order.

**Feedback:** ask students to call out the names of the months in the correct order so they can be written on the board (you could ask students to write them up).

**Teaching tip** Using the students as 'board scribes'

You can sometimes ask students to write up answers on the board. This varies the interaction pattern in the classroom, keeps students involved, and introduces an element of peer checking.

2 If your class is monolingual, this exercise can be done as a brainstorming session. Encourage students to give reasons for their answers to numbers 4, 5, and 6. Multilingual groups can work in a variety of ways: alone, in pairs, in groups, or as a brainstorming session.

**Teaching tip** Recording vocabulary

Encourage students to record vocabulary in lexical sets. They should write out the months in a separate section of their notebooks or files.

## Useful language box

**Teaching tip** Useful language

Rather than simply drawing students' attention to the language in these boxes, it may be useful to try to elicit the language from the students first, without referring to their books, in order to find out what they know. The box will then serve to consolidate what they have done in class, and as a correct reference guide.

In this case, you could write the numbers on the board, e.g. *1(st)*, *2(nd)*, and elicit the words from the students, asking them to continue as far as they can, drilling pronunciation quickly as you go. Continue in this way with the dates, highlighting the pronunciation of the weak forms, e.g. *of* /əv/, *and* /ən(d)/.

3 Students first write down four significant dates individually, then share their ideas with each other in groups. Monitor to help with any problems, and encourage students to ask more questions.

**Teaching tip** Error correction

You might like to use this exercise to point out any errors students are making. As you monitor, make a note of the errors before writing them up on the board. You can write up exactly what a student said for the class to correct. (You needn't mention who made the mistake.)

### Alternative

If your students need encouragement to speak, you could vary the dynamic within the groups by asking students to do the activity in the following way.

Write each date on a separate (small) piece of paper.

Shuffle the dates and place them face down in the centre of the group.

The students take turns to pick a piece of paper and ask what's special about that date, e.g. *What's important about the twentieth of February?*

## Numbers

1 Before students listen, discuss the pictures, making sure they know what everything is. Students can listen twice if necessary. Point out that they do not have to write down the numbers yet.

| | |
|---|---|
| 1 | a |
| 2 | d |
| 3 | c |
| 4 | e |
| 5 | b |
| 6 | e |

1 You can get me in the office on 01864 665207.
2 It's the fifth.
3 It's 147.
4 26.
5 0794 5663661.
6 The ninth of July.

2 Ask the students what information is missing in each of the pictures. For picture d ask them which date is missing. They then listen for the missing numbers. Ask the students to compare their answers in pairs if they like.

See Tapescript for answers.

3 For this exercise students can work in whatever format you like: alone, in pairs, or in groups.

1 What's your phone number?
2 What's the date today?
3 How old are you?
4 What's your mobile phone number?
5 What's your house number?
6 When's your birthday?

4 Students now listen to check their work. Play the tape / CD twice if necessary. This is a good chance to get the students practising their pronunciation of the questions before moving on to exercise 5.

1 A What's your phone number?
  B You can get me in the office on 01864 665207.
2 A What's the date today?
  B It's the fifth.
3 A How old are you?
  B 26.
4 A What's your mobile phone number?
  B 0794 5663661.
5 A What's your house number?
  B It's 147.
6 A When's your birthday?
  B The ninth of July.

5 Before doing exercise 5, draw students' attention to the tip box at the top of the margin. Students are now given the opportunity to personalize their knowledge. Move around the classroom, monitoring pronunciation.

**Feedback:** if students have taken notes, you could ask a few students to tell the class some information about their partner.

## Useful language box

Elicit the language as suggested in the **Teaching tip** on useful language earlier on this page. Briefly drill correct pronunciation as shown below.

| | |
|---|---|
| thirteen | thirty |
| fourteen | forty |
| fifteen | fifty |
| a hundred and twenty-six | and /ən(d)/ |

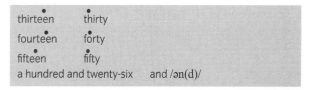

Can you remember ...?

You can use these sections before or after the **Speak out**, or as revision prompts.

## Speak out

This section features a board game for students to consolidate their work on the alphabet and different numbers. It gives students the chance to speak freely without intervention, although some help might be needed.

Make sure all the students have a counter of some sort, and demonstrate how to move around the board by tossing a coin for heads or tails. It is a good idea to allow the students to read all the questions before they begin playing, so that there are no long pauses if they come to anything they don't understand.

As students play, you can make notes on errors (see **Teaching tip** on error correction on *p.07*). Encourage them to listen to and correct each other, too. You could fit in an error correction slot immediately after students have finished, or at a later date as a form of revision.

**Feedback:** to check that students have been answering effectively, ask a number of questions at random to see how they react. They should be able to answer with little or no hesitation.

**Don't forget**

Practice exercises, Classbook, *p.76*

Teacher's Resource Pack activity 01, *ADDRESS BOOK*

# 02
## COUNTRIES & PEOPLE

## Lesson aims

- Revise and practise names of countries.
- Focus on e-mail addresses.
- Revise and practise *to be*, present and past.

## Speak for yourself

1 It is a good idea to demonstrate this exercise yourself first. See how much the students know about you, and write sentences about yourself on the board. Then refer students to the examples in the book.

2 Students read out their sentences to each other, in groups of three or four, and then see who has the longest sentence. This is a good chance for them to interact by asking each other for more information. To facilitate this, as a class activity, ask the students to think of as many questions as they can for the last sentence in exercise 1:
*I live with my wife and children in a flat in the centre of town.*

Some example questions are already given. Others could be:
*What do you think of the centre of your town?*
*What are your children's names?*
*How old are they?*

## Vocabulary

### Countries

1 Students check through the countries to see if their country is represented. If not, it can be added to the list. Go through the examples with the class to make sure they understand the idea of word stress. Then ask pairs to practise saying the countries to each other to work out where the stress falls.

**Feedback:** Put up the five stress groups on the board. Individual students say which group they think each country should go in.

| O | Oo | oO | Ooo | ooOo |
|---|-----|------|---------|----------|
| France | Russia | Brazil | Mexico | Argentina |
| Spain | Turkey | Japan | Portugal | |
| Greece | China | | Germany | |
| | Sweden | | Hungary | |
| | Poland | | Italy | |

### Extra

You could follow this up by doing a geography quiz, testing students' knowledge of the countries in exercise 1. This will give students the opportunity to practise saying the countries with the correct stress. Put the students into teams of three or four. Give the capitals of the countries one by one (in random order) and tell the groups to check together and then raise their hand if they are sure they know the country. Give the first team to raise their hand one point for the correct country and one point for the correct pronunciation. If a team gives an incorrect answer, the second team to raise their hand can win a bonus point by giving the correct answer.

| Brasilia | **Brazil** | Madrid | **Spain** |
|----------|-----------|--------|-----------|
| Mexico City | **Mexico** | Budapest | **Hungary** |
| Paris | **France** | Beijing | **China** |
| Lisbon | **Portugal** | Stockholm | **Sweden** |
| Berlin | **Germany** | Rome | **Italy** |
| Moscow | **Russia** | Warsaw | **Poland** |
| Ankara | **Turkey** | Tokyo | **Japan** |
| Buenos Aires | **Argentina** | Athens | **Greece** |

2 To show they have understood the word stress, students can suggest other countries and say which stress group they go in.

Focus students on the box in the margin. Elicit how to say '@' (*at*) and '.' (*dot*). You could either ask students to discuss in pairs before giving their answers to the class, or do this as a class activity.

| monica ... | Brazil | peter ... | Australia |
|------------|--------|-----------|-----------|
| elizabeth ... | Russia | msantos ... | Portugal |
| hunter ... | Greece | | |

### Extra

You could follow up by asking students to dictate their own e-mail addresses to a partner or group.

### EXPAND your vocabulary

Students can do this activity in pairs or groups. Tell them to use a dictionary to check their answers. You can ask students to complete the list for the countries in exercise 1 in class or for homework, but make sure they know how to write and say their own nationalities. Remind students to record new vocabulary (see **Teaching tip** on recording vocabulary on *p.07*).

| **Japan** | Japanese |
|-----------|----------|
| **Germany** | German |
| **Brazil** | Brazilian |

**Teaching tip** Student autonomy

Encourage students to use their dictionaries as a resource which will enable them to be more independent learners (some learners need no encouragement!). Demonstrate here how they can use English–English dictionaries to expand their vocabulary, and point out how pronunciation is shown (stress and phonetic symbols) if you feel they can cope with this at this stage.

## Grammar

### *to be*, present and past

**Note**

The unfamiliar vocabulary in the texts is likely to be:

**Marzia's e-mail**
old people's home, a monster, never mind

**Jim's e-mail**
glad, believe it or not, misty, ago

1 Students read through the e-mails quietly. Alternatively, one of the students or you can read them out.

2 Students close their books and write down what they can remember.

3 In groups, students read out their ideas to each other, checking for accuracy. Tell them that they can ask you if in doubt.

4 Students read the texts again and highlight the relevant grammar. Do one example of each tense in class first.

   **Feedback:** ask students to compare their answers in pairs and then as a class.

| present | past |
| --- | --- |
| my name's | I was |
| I'm (x2) | we were |
| it's | the weather wasn't |
| the pay is | it was (x2) |
| the hours are | the people were |
| my boss is | it wasn't |
| | we were |

Focus students on the box in the margin (*ago*). Ask a few students the example questions to check understanding. Briefly drill one or two of the example questions. If they need more practice, ask them to write two more questions in pairs, using *ago*, to ask other students.

## Grammar box: *to be*, present and past

Refer students to the language box before they do the **Practice** section. Alternatively, you could elicit the language as suggested in the **Teaching tip** on useful language on *p.07*.

## Practice

1 This can be a class activity. Ask the students to tell you how many sentences must go in the past and why. They should identify key phrases such as *in 1974*.

| | |
| --- | --- |
| 2 | in 1974 |
| 3 | two weeks ago |
| 6 | yesterday |
| 7 | last year |
| 4 | could go in the past if the current month follows July, i.e. if it is between August and December. |

2 Students fill in the sentences as appropriate. You can demonstrate this first by making the sentences true for you.

3 Students work together and exchange information. Monitor accuracy. This can also be followed up with a general question and answer session in class, e.g. *What do you do? When were you born? When was your last holiday?*

### Alternative

Ask students to write four sentences about themselves using *to be*, two in the present and two in the past. They should include one sentence which is not true. Ask them to get into groups of three or four and read their sentences to the group. The group should decide which sentence is not true. If they guess correctly they ask questions to find out the true information. If not they continue guessing. For example:

| Student A | Group |
| --- | --- |
| *I was born in 1974.* | *That's not true.* |
| *You're right. It's not true.* | *When were you born?* |
| *I was born in 1970.* | |

Demonstrate this first by giving the class four sentences about yourself.

4 Divide the class into teams. The number in each team is not important. Each team then works on their famous names. Make sure that no teams have the same names.

   You can award points if you wish. A suggested system is two points for the correct answer. If a team answer incorrectly, the question can be passed to another team, who get a bonus point.

### Teaching tip  Classroom management

To decide who starts, think of a number between 0 and 100, then ask each team to think of a number in the same range. The team with the number nearest to yours begins.

### Can you remember ...?

You can use these sections before or after the **Speak out**, or as revision prompts.

## Speak out

1 Students work alone, and write a short e-mail similar to Marzia's and Jim's. Before they begin, ask them if they remember the topics of the e-mails, and write them up on the board, e.g.

| Name | Last holiday – where |
| --- | --- |
| Where from | Weather |
| Occupation | Food |
| Where living | People |

Ensure they include information about the present and the past to ensure full coverage of the verb *to be*. You could give students a time limit of about ten minutes for this activity.

2 Students now get into pairs and exchange e-mails.

3 In groups, students report back on their partner's e-mail. They should do this without referring to the text if they can. If you feel your students are a particularly strong group, you can take away the e-mails. Otherwise, allow them to look if they have problems.

### Alternative

If you have a small class, you can ask students to write their e-mails in the same way, but omitting their names. When everyone has finished, collect them in and shuffle them. Hand them out to the class, making sure nobody has their own. Ask students to report back on the e-mail they have been given, as in exercise 3. The rest of the class has to guess who wrote the e-mail. This also gives you a chance to monitor any problems that individuals are having.

### Don't forget

Practice exercises, Classbook *p.77*

Teacher's Resource Pack activity 02, *WISH YOU WERE HERE*

# 03
## FRIENDS & RELATIONS

## Lesson aims

- Revise, extend, and practise family vocabulary.
- Introduce vocabulary to describe homes and houses.
- Revise and practise *have got / has got*.
- Give students the opportunity to talk about where they, their friends, and their family live.

## Vocabulary challenge

### Note  The family

Students are expected to know quite a few members of the family. The beginning of this lesson aims to consolidate this knowledge, confirm the vocabulary that they can probably guess, and extend their vocabulary.

1  Do this as a speed challenge. Find out which student can identify the three categories first, before asking the meanings of new words.

### Alternative

If you feel your class needs help, draw a three-column table on the board, as below. Call out family words individually and ask students to put them into the columns, using red, blue, and green board pens if possible. Leave a space opposite the male and female words to be filled in with the other word in the pair later (shown in brackets in the key).

If you feel pronunciation may be a problem, ask the students to call out the words, and confirm or correct as you write them on the board.

| Exercises 1 and 2 | | |
| --- | --- | --- |
| male (red) | female (blue) | both (green) |
| father | (mother) | parent |
| grandson | (granddaughter) | |
| grandfather | (grandmother) | |
| uncle | (aunt) | |
| boyfriend | (girlfriend) | |
| brother | (sister) | |
| (husband) | wife | spouse |
| (son) | daughter | child |
| (nephew) | niece | |
| (ex-husband) | ex-wife | |
| (father-in-law) | mother-in-law | |
| | | cousin |

2  This should be a very quick activity. Students work in pairs, preferably sitting opposite each other. Student A can test the male words, Student B the female words. They can then swap over and test each other again, if need be. Monitor for unknown words and pronunciation. Students should draw up their own table of family words, using the headings *male*, *female*, and *both* in the vocabulary section of their notebooks.

### Alternative

If you feel that students won't know the male / female equivalent, you can get them to complete the table which is already on the board (see exercise 1, **Alternative**).

Refer students to the tip box in the margin. Focus on the use of the possessive *'s* to talk about families.

3  In groups of three or four, students talk about three of their relations. Introduce the activity by referring to the example or giving one or two of your own. Be available to help with language.

### Teaching tip  Realia

If you have photos of your own family to make the activity more immediate, all the better. You may find that students carry photos of their family with them. Encourage students to show them to each other as they talk.

Other topics where your photos would be useful to stimulate interest and discussion include: your holidays, your friends, your flat / house, photos of you taken over the years (with different clothes / hairstyles, in different places).

## Grammar
### *have got / has got*

### Teaching tip  Scanning

In texts like this unfamiliar vocabulary may worry some students. It is important that they should be encouraged to realize that they can understand the main points in a text without understanding every word. Equally, many words will become clear from the context.

Make sure that students understand the vocabulary in the sentences in exercise 1. However, other unfamiliar vocabulary should probably not be focused on until the end of the activity. Where possible, encourage students to use each other as a resource, using the question *What does 'x' mean?*

Use English–English dictionaries to find any remaining unknown words.

### Note

The unfamiliar vocabulary is likely to be:
die(d), space, heating, comfortable, unfortunately, view, island, rents, suburbs, nearby

1  Demonstrate this activity yourself to make sure that students understand the instructions, particularly *true* and *false*. Students work alone, then compare ideas with a partner or in small groups.

2  Focus students on the first sentence and ask them to read the first paragraph of the text to find out why the sentence is false (*It was a small house for seven people*). Students work alone first, then check with a partner.

**Feedback:** whole class. Give students the opportunity to give reasons and to quote from the text. Encourage the use of phrases like *It's true / false because it / she says …*

---

**Teaching tip** Annotating text

Encourage students to interact with the text. Ask them to underline and number the sections of text that provide them with their answer. This means that they can easily refer back to the section of text that confirms their answers, and also emphasizes the fact that, for that particular task, the rest of the text with any unknown words is unimportant. Coloured highlighters are highly recommended, so that in this text, for example, past could be pink and present green.

When it comes to finding rooms and parts of the house (see exercise 3), they can circle them or put an asterisk.

---

3 **Against the clock.** Students do this within the time limit, and then compare with a partner.

living room    bedroom    bathroom    kitchen    balcony
top floor

4 Students can work alone, in pairs or in groups, to put their own ideas into the spidergram. Elicit a few examples from the class first. It may be useful for them to copy the spidergram into their vocabulary books before filling it in.

**Feedback:** copy the spidergram onto the board (or an OHT). Appoint a scribe for each room on the spidergram, and ask other students to call out their words. Remind the scribes to ask *How do you spell that?* Alternatively, you could write up the words called out by students, checking spelling as you go. Possible answers are suggested, but accept alternatives.

**Possible answers**

| living room | kitchen | bedroom | bathroom |
|---|---|---|---|
| armchairs | cooker | bed | toilet |
| sofa | fridge | chest of | basin |
| coffee table | (refrigerator) | drawers | bath |
| television | cupboards | wardrobe | shower |
| bookcase | dishwasher | bedside | bidet |
| | freezer | tables | |

## Alternative

You could make this activity more competitive. Divide the class into a maximum of four teams. Set a time limit of about five minutes. Students have to brainstorm and write down as many things as they can which may be found in the four rooms. Meanwhile, draw a large spidergram on the board. When time is up, the four team captains (with their teams behind them in a line) stand side by side in front of the board. Each team has a different coloured board pen or piece of chalk. When you call *Start*, students work in relay to write as many words on the board as they can, one at a time. If another team has already written their word, they can't write it again. Team members can help with spelling. Call *Stop* after an agreed time and count the number of words each team has written up. You decide how hard you want to be on spelling, although it's probably a good idea to start as you mean to go on.

5 Students identify examples of *have got / has got* in the text. Make sure students underline complete phrases using the verb.

**Feedback:** whole class. Elicit the verbs and confirm the whole phrase, using questions such as *What has her house got? What hasn't she got?*

it's got a big living room
it's got lots of space
we've got heating
my mother's house hasn't (negative)
we haven't got a very good view (negative)
she hasn't got air-conditioning (negative)

## Grammar box: *have got / has got*

Refer students to the grammar box (*have got / has got*) and point out that Rita uses the short forms of the verb (*it's got / we've got*). Elicit the long forms.

## Practice

1 Introduce this exercise with a few examples about you and / or elicit a few from the students. Students now complete the sentences with the appropriate form of *have got*. Make sure they understand that the sentences should then be true. This should produce a variety of forms, including *have / has got* and *haven't / hasn't got*. Refer students to the grammar box for the correct spelling and forms.

**Feedback:** check students' answers and help with any problems.

2 This exercise is designed to test students' grasp of word order. Point out the difference between statements and questions.

**Feedback:** whole class. It might be worth writing the questions on the board to ensure that everyone has the correct answers.

1 How many brothers and sisters have you got?
2 Has your house got air-conditioning?
3 Have you got a CD player?
4 Have you got any nephews and nieces?
5 How much free time have you got?
6 Have you got a flat or a house?

---

**Note** Articles

Check the students understand the use of articles in the questions in exercise 2, e.g. *a* (singular: *CD player*, *flat*, *house*), *any* (plural: *nephews and nieces*), and no article (uncountable: *air-conditioning*). *Any* can also be used for uncountable nouns, e.g. *Has your house got any air-conditioning?*

---

3 In pairs, students now ask each other the questions in exercise 2. You may wish to practise sentence stress first in class, marking the stressed words in each question.

## Extra

If you feel your students need further practice of question formation, ask students to write more questions to ask other students using *Have you got...?* and *How much / many ... have you got?* If your students need ideas you could give them prompts, e.g. *a bicycle, a motorbike, a car, a holiday home, cousins, in-laws, money in your purse*. By giving them prompts you can also make sure they ask questions using *a*, *any*, and no article.

# English in use

## Where do you live?

---

**Note** British and American English

The first speaker in the listening is English, and the second is American. This is a good opportunity to point out that there are certain differences in spelling and vocabulary between British and American English. It is important that students are aware of this, and that they don't see either as wrong.

---

1 Refer students to the box in the margin. If you have time you could elicit more differences between British and American English. Students listen to two people speaking about their homes and note down key words in the table.

........................................................

**Diana**

I live in a **house** in a **village** near Oxford. It's about **80** years old and made of **stone**. We've got a living room, study, dining room, and kitchen downstairs. Upstairs there are three **bedrooms** and two **bathrooms** – one of them is en suite. I think my favourite room has to be our bedroom – it has a view of the **garden** and the **hills** beyond. My husband and I love gardening, so we spend a lot of time outside in the summer.

**Shawn**

My apartment is on the **third** floor of an old **wooden** house. It's **pretty** big for **one person**, but that's good. It's got two bedrooms and a very large living room, which is great for me because I travel a lot and bring lots of things home with me. There's a small kitchen with a balcony leading off of it, and a decent bathroom. My favorite room's the **living room**. That's where I **watch** TV and **listen** to music. It's also where the **air-conditioning** is – it gets hot in Boston in the summer.

Feedback: whole class.

|  | Diana | Shawn |
|---|---|---|
| **where** | a village near Oxford | Boston |
| **who with** | husband | alone |
| **rooms** | living room, study, dining room, kitchen, three bedrooms, two bathrooms | two bedrooms, living room, kitchen and balcony, bathroom |
| **favourite room** | bedroom | living room |

---

**Teaching tip** Listening for specific information

As with reading, it is essential that students learn to focus on what is important for the task and ignore what is irrelevant. If students are finding it difficult, you can do the first couple of questions with them. Ask them *Where does Diana live?* and play the tape / CD. Students should call out *Stop* when they hear the answer to the question.

---

2 Alone or in pairs, students try to remember who said which phrases. Don't be afraid to let students listen again if they're struggling. Again it may be a good idea to let students stop the tape / CD when they hear the phrases.

See Tapescript for answers.

3 Students listen again to check their answers, then practise the phrases. This can be done as a class in chorus, or with a partner.

4 Students complete the sentences from memory, alone or in pairs. If students work alone, give them an opportunity to compare their answers before checking with the Tapescript.

See Tapescript for answers.

### Alternative

Half of the class can complete Diana's sentences, and half Shawn's. When they have finished, they check their own answers with the Tapescript and then test each other's memory, with a whistle dictation.

---

**Teaching tip** Whistle dictation

Read a gapped sentence or text aloud, whistling in place of the missing word. Students must try to fill in the gap.

---

5 This exercise gives students the opportunity to work alone with language from the lesson. Whilst trying to personalize the language, students will be able to see what they have and perhaps haven't understood, and will probably want to check their understanding with you or their peers. They shouldn't, however, spend more than ten minutes on the writing.

Feedback: ask students to hand in their writing for you to correct. In pairs, students proofread each other's work, before you have the final word. You can then ask them to write the correct version on cards to stick up on a notice board or make into a class poster.

### Can you remember ...?

You can use these sections before or after the **Speak out**, or as revision prompts.

## Speak out

1 This gives students the opportunity to think about where their family and friends live before they actually have to talk about one or two people (in exercise 2).

2 Give students time to check vocabulary with you, their peers, or a dictionary before they start speaking. Encourage them to plan what they are going to say, e.g. by making notes, but make sure they don't write everything down. Monitor as they speak in pairs or groups, but don't interrupt.

Feedback: make sure you are positive about students' speaking, referring to content rather than language. Make sure the lesson ends on a high, rather than discouraging them with a catalogue of mistakes.

---

**Teaching tip** Error correction

Concentrate on errors connected with the lesson, in this case *have got / has got*, and the vocabulary of family and homes. It may be a good idea to do error correction in a subsequent lesson. On an OHT or on the board, write a list of errors and ask students for suggested improvements. If students recognize their own errors, give them the opportunity to correct themselves.

---

**Don't forget**

Practice exercises, Classbook *p.78*

Teacher's Resource Pack activity 03a, *HAVE YOU GOT ...?*

Teacher's Resource Pack activity 03b, *A ROOM OF MY OWN*

---

# 04
## LIFE & ROUTINE

## What do you know?

1   Students write as many sentences as they can. You could set a time limit of three minutes if you like. Before they begin, point out the example. If necessary, ask the class for another example with a different verb.

| I get | I get up at 7.00. I get the bus to work. |
|---|---|
| I have | I have a shower. I have a sandwich for lunch. |
| I go | I go to bed at about 11.00. I go home straight after work. I go to a café for breakfast. |
| I work | I work from nine to five. I work hard! I work in an office. |
| **Alternatives** | |
| I get a sandwich for lunch. | |
| I get home straight after work. | |

2   Demonstrate the activity before asking students to tick the sentences that are true for them.

3   Students discuss their answers in groups. This is also a chance for students to question each other further, and to introduce the question form of the present simple. If somebody doesn't get up at 7.00, encourage students to ask *What time do you get up?*

## Vocabulary
### Daily routines

1   **Against the clock.** Give students three minutes to do this exercise alone, in pairs, or in groups. The advantage of working in pairs or groups is that they will come up with a greater range of vocabulary.

Go through the examples. Point out the use of a whole phrase with *office*. The key below shows possible answers, but students will certainly have alternatives.

**Possible answers**
have a sandwich, ride a bike, work in an office, buy a paper, watch TV, go out with friends, have lunch, go to a café, have a shower, catch the bus, eat in a restaurant, go to bed, have dinner, go to the gym, have a coffee, have a bath

**Feedback:** write up students' ideas on the board. This will be useful for exercise 2.

### Alternative

To vary class dynamics, ask students to close their books. Call out each word, and tell students to write down a corresponding verb or phrase. Then go through the answers.

2   Students now listen to three people discussing their daily routine. They should listen for any expressions they came up with in exercise 1.
**Feedback:** ask students to come up to the board and tick any expressions they have heard.

Students listen again and complete the gaps. If they are having problems, they can ask you to stop the tape / CD (see **Teaching tip** on listening for specific information on *p.13*).
**Feedback:** students read out their answers to the class.

See Tapescript for answers.

1   I usually **get up** at about 6.30. I just **have coffee** for breakfast. I **get the bus** to work. If I'm late I **take a taxi**, which is a bit expensive. My wife **goes by bike**, she likes to keep fit.
2   I always **go to the gym** at lunchtimes, about 12.30 or 12.45. I **have a shower** there too, and I often **go to the café** for lunch.
3   I **leave the office** at around 6.00 and maybe **meet some friends** for a drink. I don't **watch much telly**, too much to do, and I never **go to bed** before midnight.

### Alternative

Get different students to come up and write one sentence each on the board. Other students discuss whether the sentences are correct.

3   Focus students on the clocks and ask them what time each clock says. With a stronger class you could draw the clocks on the board and elicit the words directly from the students.

### Extra

You may wish to expand this exercise by asking students *What time is it?* and practising the answer *It's …*

If students need more practice, you could do a time dictation.

**Time dictation**
Ask students to draw four clocks on a piece of paper, all showing different times (ideally practising the four target words, *o'clock, quarter past, quarter to, half past*). When they have done this, they draw four blank clocks on the same piece of paper. Ask them to work in pairs and not to look at each other's pieces of paper. Student A asks *What time is it?* Student B gives the time on the first clock. Student A then draws the time described by Student B in the first blank clock. Student B then asks the same question and has to draw in the time described by Student A in the first blank clock. They continue in this way until they have filled in the four blank clocks described by their partner. When they have finished, they can compare their clocks to check their answers. This can be consolidated by asking the students to write the times beneath the clocks, either in class or for homework.

## Grammar
### Present simple

1   Students work alone. They might ask for help, but at this stage it is probably better to let them work as independently as possible to see how much they know.

**2** Students check their answers together. If there are any disagreements you can intervene here.

Feedback: individual students can read out their answers.

| | |
|---|---|
| 1 works | 6 does / do |
| 2 do / read | 7 work |
| 3 go / don't like | 8 goes |
| 4 doesn't drink | 9 do / live or work |
| 5 takes | 10 don't watch |

**Teaching tip** Feedback

When students discuss their answers in class, give them the option of answering any question they like, not necessarily in order. They are then not forced into the corner of answering a question they found difficult.

## Grammar box: Present simple

Focus students on the grammar box or elicit the forms of the present simple, as suggested in the **Teaching tip** on useful language on *p.07*.

## Practice

**1** Students correct the mistakes in each sentence, working alone or in pairs.

1 I phone her every day.
2 We don't / do not work at the weekend.
3 How do you get home?
4 I start work at nine o'clock.
5 She doesn't drive to work.
6 Do they like living in the United States?
7 Do you always have a sandwich for lunch?
8 Does this bus go to the city centre?

**2** Focus students' attention on the language box in the margin. You could give a few examples about yourself before asking students to write their own sentences.

Feedback: students can compare their sentences in pairs or groups. You could ask them if they found any information surprising.

### Extra

You could use the students' sentences using *every* for extra question and answer practice by doing a student generated *Find someone who …* Their sentences would have to be about themselves.

Student generated *Find someone who …*
When students have written their sentences, collect them in, shuffle them, and put them face down in a pile on your desk. Ask the students to get up, take a piece of paper each, and read the information on it. They then have to try to guess who the sentences were written by. They approach this person and ask direct questions to confirm their guesses. If it is clear that they are not speaking to the right person, they should move on. They continue asking questions about the five sentences until they are absolutely sure they are speaking to the person who wrote the sentences. They can then put the paper back at the bottom of the pile and take another one. This can continue until most of the students have found at least one person. For example:
(Student A's sentence) *I go for a walk every weekend.*
(Student B's question) *Do you go for a walk every weekend?*
(Student A's response) *Yes, I do.*

### Note

The unfamiliar vocabulary in exercise 3 is likely to be: midnight, lock, relaxing, a pet, a horror story

**3** Allow students time to read through the text. Go through any problem vocabulary. Students then discuss their routines in pairs.

Feedback: ask a few students about their partner's routine.

**Teaching tip** Guessing vocabulary from context

Ask students not to look up the unfamiliar words in their dictionaries but to try to guess them from the context. It is a good idea to let students discuss the words in pairs before you ask the class for their ideas.

### Extra

Students choose their top three most helpful tips. They then discuss their ideas in groups.

### Can you remember …?

You can use these sections before or after the **Speak out**, or as revision prompts.

## Speak out

**1** It is perhaps best to start this activity by giving students a short summary of your routine and how you feel about it. Do you sometimes feel like a robot? Students then get into pairs and discuss their routines. Encourage them to use language covered in this lesson. Refer them to the **Can you remember …?** box to refresh their memories first.

### Alternative

Ask the students to think of some questions they might like to ask you about your daily life. Answer their questions and deal with any problems. They can then ask their partner the same questions, e.g. *What time do you get up? What do you have for breakfast?*

**2** In groups, students talk about their partner's routine, and go on to discuss who seems to have the most interesting or unusual lifestyle. Go round helping students who might need extra vocabulary.

Feedback: this would be another opportunity to collect any mistakes to look at after the activity, or at a later date.

**Teaching tip** Error correction

Deciding when to analyse mistakes with students is not easy. After an activity like this **Speak out**, it might be better to leave students with the feeling of having communicated successfully. On the other hand, looking at their mistakes in a subsequent lesson will make the language concerned less immediate. Time may well be a factor, but otherwise let the mood of your students decide you.

**Don't forget**

Practice exercises, Classbook p.80

Teacher's Resource Pack activity 04, *ARE YOU A GOOD STUDENT?*

- Give students the opportunity to talk about people and where they live.
- Practise the present simple third person.
- Practise adverbs of frequency.

## Vocabulary challenge

1 For this exercise, students can work alone, in pairs, or in groups. To motivate students, you can do this as a race. The first to finish should call out or put up their hand, and then read out their answers to the class. Other students listen and check. There should be discussion about which adjective should go where, e.g. *horrible* could go in all three categories.

| people | food | weather |
|---|---|---|
| friendly | delicious | freezing |
| horrible | tasty | horrible |
| interesting | horrible | wet |
| relaxed | salty | sunny |
| caring | expensive | hot |
| boring | hot | beautiful |
| beautiful | boring | |

### Extra

To extend students' knowledge of adjectives further, ask them to find opposites in the list. They should suggest:

| | |
|---|---|
| interesting | boring |
| sunny | wet |
| freezing | hot |

Ask them to look at the other adjectives, and think of opposites.

| Possible answers | |
|---|---|
| delicious / tasty | disgusting |
| friendly | unfriendly |
| horrible | nice |
| relaxed | stressed |
| caring | uncaring |
| expensive | cheap |
| beautiful | ugly |
| salty | sweet |

2 Students get into groups to discuss the people, food, and weather in their countries.

## English in use
### Describing your life

### Note
The unfamiliar vocabulary in the texts is likely to be:

**Mongolia**
bright, colleagues, extremely, health, eating habits, social life, popular

**Solomon Islands**
leaf, repair, breeze, tranquillity, insects, imported

1 **Against the clock.** Give the students one minute to read the texts alone so that they do not get bogged down in the detail. At this stage students are simply meant to scan the text for the correct answers.

**Feedback:** students might like to work in pairs or groups to compare answers before reporting back to the class. Encourage them to point out the parts of the text that gave them their ideas.

Becky is a teacher (probably an English teacher) in Mongolia. She seems to enjoy her work (*very interesting ... I never know what will happen next*). Ruth is also a teacher (again probably an English teacher) in the Solomon Islands. It's not clear whether she enjoys her work – she seems to enjoy living there, but the job doesn't sound easy.

2 Focus students on the good and bad things in the texts. Then ask them to read the texts again, as this activity requires more detailed understanding than exercise 1. As they read, ask them to write down any problem vocabulary, which can then be discussed in class.

**Feedback:** whole class. Put two columns on the board, *Good things* and *Bad things*, and write up students' ideas as they mention them. You can also use the students as board scribes.

**Mongolia**
**Good things**
her work is interesting
her colleagues are friendly, caring, and good fun
the weather – it almost never rains
**Bad things**
the cold
the distance from other places, so she doesn't see her friends back home very often
horse's milk and salty tea
**Solomon Islands**
**Good things**
the sunny mornings
the tranquillity and the relaxed atmosphere
the friendly people
the kids
the family she lives with
**Bad things**
the insects
the waiting
the heat
imported food is expensive
she's a bit bored with local food

### Teaching tip   Peer teaching

Get students to compare their lists of problem vocabulary in pairs or groups of three. They might be able to help each other, reducing the amount of time needed to explain things in class. Class explanations can frustrate students who already know the vocabulary.

3 Students work alone for this exercise. Ask the students where Becky and Ruth work (Becky in Mongolia and Ruth in the Solomon Islands).

Emphasize that, where possible, they should find a suitable point in the text to confirm their ideas.

| 1 | Ruth | *There's a lovely breeze coming from the sea 100 metres away.* |
|---|---|---|
| 2 | Ruth | Becky teaches university students. |
| 3 | Becky | Mongolia is bordered by these two countries. |
| 4 | Ruth | *There's a lovely breeze coming from the sea 100 metres away.* |
| 5 | Ruth | The Solomon Islands are much more likely to have fresh fruit than Mongolia. |
| 6 | Becky | *The temperature is sometimes around −20ºC in winter …* |
| 7 | Becky | *All the people I work with are extremely friendly …* |
| 8 | Ruth | *The insects …* |
| 9 | Becky | *… I only see my friends once a year.* |
| 10 | Becky | *… it almost never rains.* |

## Grammar box: Present simple spelling – *he / she / it*

Draw students' attention to the spelling box or elicit the third person forms and write them on the board.

4   Students can work alone here, checking the sentences in exercise 3 for examples of the spelling patterns. To speed up the exercise, you can ask for the first student who finishes to call out.

   **Feedback:** students read out their answers to the class, who act as judges.

| 1 | washes, dries | 4 | goes, finishes |
|---|---|---|---|
| 2 | teaches | 7 | goes |
| 3 | studies | 9 | misses |

5   Once again, it is probably best to have students working alone at first.

   **Feedback:** give students the opportunity to check in pairs before going through the answers with the whole class.

| 1 | misses | 4 | study |
|---|---|---|---|
| 2 | go | 5 | washes |
| 3 | dries | | |

---

**Teaching tip**   Working alone

It is useful to ask students to work alone at first on appropriate activities in each lesson, as this gives you a chance to monitor and to spot anybody having difficulties. If possible avoid helping or correcting, as you can get students to compare answers in pairs or groups once they have finished. This gives them a chance to teach each other and to reinforce their learning.

---

6   In pairs, students listen to the sentences, but only write down the verbs they hear. At this stage check their work, and replay the sentences so they can now concentrate on the pronunciation of each individual verb. They now practise the pronunciation in pairs. One student points at a verb, the other says it. You can move around the classroom, listening and helping out with any difficulties.

   The second stage of the activity is to see if the students can now write down the whole of each sentence from memory. Play the sentences again so that they can check their work. You can also ask the students to read the sentences out loud to give them more pronunciation practice.

See Tapescript for answers.

🔊 1

1   She **teaches** university students.
2   She **goes** to work at 8.30.
3   She **washes** her hair every morning.
4   She **studies** French and German.
5   She **misses** her family.

### Alternative

If students are finding it difficult to remember the complete sentences, you can approach the activity in a different way, using Cuisenaire rods if possible. Put students into pairs and give each pair more rods than the complete number of words in the longest sentence. Play the first sentence and ask the pairs to place a rod in front of them for each word in the sentence. Contractions count as two words. When they are ready ask the class how many words there are in the sentence. If there is disagreement, let them listen again before checking the sentence with them. If you feel they need practice with word stress and linking, you can ask them to raise the rods for the stressed words, and / or put rods together for words which are linked. In order to do this students have to say the sentences out loud to each other. The visual aid can help to focus students' attention on the details of each sentence. After doing this it will be simple for students to write the sentences down, if you feel this is necessary.

Students may find this strange if they are doing it for the first time, so take them through the first sentence carefully before asking them to continue with the rest of the sentences.

## Grammar
### Adverbs of frequency

1   Students can work alone or in pairs.

   **Feedback:** you can either have students reading their sentences out in class, or have them checking in the texts to find the answers for themselves. The first gives them pronunciation practice, the latter allows them to reinforce their reading.

| 1 | often | 4 | sometimes |
|---|---|---|---|
| 2 | always | 5 | hardly ever |
| 3 | never | 6 | usually |

2   Ask students to discuss this in pairs.

   **Feedback:** copy the chart onto the board and write up their ideas, or use the students as scribes. They may ask you for percentages if they feel unclear about any of the adverbs. Let the class decide as far as possible.

always, usually, often, sometimes, hardly ever, never

3   Students work alone. You could demonstrate the activity by writing the numbers 1 to 8 on the board and ticking the numbers which are true for you.

   **Feedback:** it might be interesting to find out which student has ticked the most sentences.

4   Students change their sentences alone. Go through the example first, or demonstrate by using yourself as an example again. Move around helping with any difficulties.

5   Students now work in pairs. Encourage them to ask as many questions as possible. Join in their conversations, asking questions of your own. You can also tell them about some of your own habits.

**Feedback:** you could follow this up with an error correction activity, focusing on the use of the present simple and adverbs of frequency.

## Alternative

In order to vary the dynamic of exercise 5 you could tell students to guess which sentences their partner has ticked. If they are wrong, they should ask questions or guess how their partner has corrected the sentences, e.g. (Student A) *I think you always have a cup of tea first thing in the morning.* (Student B) *That's true. I think you hardly ever go to the beach at the weekend.* (Student A) *That's not true. I usually go to the beach at the weekend if it's sunny.*

### Teaching tip Error correction

It is a good idea to focus on the target language in an activity like this. In order to make sure the error correction is a positive activity for the students, you can collect examples of good language as well as useful mistakes. You can deal with this in two ways. Put two columns on the board, with a tick at the top of one and a cross at the top of the other. Write the good language in the first column and the errors in the second, asking the students to look at the columns, copy any good language into their books, and correct the errors in pairs.

When they are ready, go through the errors with the class and congratulate them on the good language. Alternatively, with a strong class, you can show the students both the good and incorrect language (with no distinction) and ask pairs to decide which sentences or phrases are correct and incorrect, before correcting the mistakes. If they are finding this difficult, go through it as a class.

## Can you remember ...?

You can use these sections before or after the **Speak out**, or as revision prompts.

# Speak out

1 Copy the headings of the table onto the board (*Routine, Good things, Bad things*). Ask the students to recap this information about Becky and Ruth orally in pairs. If they need help, tell them to read the texts again quickly.

Now direct their attention to foreign English language teachers in their own country. Elicit one similarity and one difference to the lives Becky and Ruth lead. Put these on the board.

Point out the topics suggested for good and bad things in the book, and encourage students to suggest their own topics. Draw attention to the example sentences in the table. Students should now write similar sentences drawing on their own knowledge. Some imagination might be needed, but this is fine. As the students write their sentences, move around correcting and helping out with any difficulties. In a monolingual class, students could begin by working alone or in pairs. In a multilingual class students from the same country could work together to pool their ideas.

2 Put students into groups so that they can compare and discuss their ideas. Split up students who have worked together in exercise 1. In a multilingual class, form groups containing students from a variety of countries and tell them to find the similarities and differences. Join in with the discussions and add your own ideas. You may be in a good position to agree or disagree with any observations. You can also use the activity to note down any mistakes to use in class afterwards, or at a later date.

**Feedback:** once the students have finished their group discussions, it is a good idea to pool their ideas in class, so conclusions can be drawn. Ask students for their ideas, and write them up in the table on the board. Students will now discover from other groups things they hadn't thought of themselves.

## Extra

You could take advantage of this topic to give students the opportunity to use English in an authentic way outside the classroom. Tell them to conduct a survey among the English teachers at their school in order to find out about their experiences in different countries. They would have to compile a list of questions, interview several teachers, and take notes. In a subsequent class students could report back to the class on their findings.

**Don't forget**

Practice exercises, Classbook, *p.82*

Teacher's Resource Pack activity 05a, *TELL US ABOUT YOUR COUNTRY*

Teacher's Resource Pack activity 05b, *WHOSE ROUTINES?*

# 06
## JOBS & WORK

### Lesson aims

- Introduce and practise vocabulary for jobs and occupations.
- Focus on job advertisements.
- Practise talking about what you and other people do.

## Speak for yourself

### Note

Unfamiliar vocabulary is likely to be:
salary, outdoors, team

1 Students work alone. Before they begin, check students understand the vocabulary by going through the list of things.

### Extra

In pairs, encourage the students to find opposites for each of the criteria. There are no right or wrong answers, so accept as many ideas as possible. This will give them a wider range of vocabulary and broaden the base for discussion in exercise 2.

| Possible answers | |
|---|---|
| a good salary | a low salary |
| working alone | working in a team |
| lots of travel | staying in one place |
| long holidays | short holidays |
| working outdoors | working indoors |
| working in an office | working at home |
| an interesting routine | a boring routine |
| being the boss | working for someone |

2 In pairs, students compare their ideas. Monitor their discussions, helping where necessary. Make a note of any vocabulary students need. This can be brought to the attention of the class at the end of the activity.

### Alternative

Ask students to keep their books closed and to come up with their own ideas of what constitutes a good job, in pairs. This combines exercises 1 and 2. Give them a maximum of five minutes. Move around the classroom helping them with any difficult vocabulary.

When they have finished, ask two students to come to the board. The rest of the class call out their findings, and the two students take it in turns to write these up on the board. Finally, the class compare their ideas with the list in exercise 1 in the book.

### Teaching tip  Class dynamics

Mix students up when putting them in pairs. Generally, students quickly work out who they want to sit next to, but it is a good idea to break these patterns now and again. It helps class cohesion and creates variety.

## Vocabulary

### Occupations

1 This is a class activity. Point students to the example in the book, highlighting the different answers to the question *What do you do?* or use yourself as an example, e.g. *I'm a teacher. I work for XX School.*

Draw students' attention to the language box in the margin. You could check understanding by putting a few jobs on the board and asking *a* or *an*?

At this stage, either ask the students to write down two ways of answering the question for themselves, or move around the class, asking individual students the question. This approach is more spontaneous, but some students might have problems expressing what they do. Writing gives the students more time to think about the language. They can also look to you for help. Of course, you can ask the students to read out their work at the end.

### Alternative

With a stronger group, you can simply ask students at random what they do. If they just name their job, ask them for more details by asking them where they work, or where they study.

2 **Against the clock.** Working alone, give students two minutes to match the pictures with the jobs. Avoid helping anybody, as the students will have a chance to help each other in the feedback session.

**Feedback:** put the students in pairs to compare answers. It is quite a good idea to pair strong and weak students, thus giving students the opportunity to learn from each other (see **Teaching tip** on peer teaching on *p.16*). Finally, check the answers as a class.

| | | | |
|---|---|---|---|
| lawyer | 4 | builder | 10 |
| teacher | 7 | photographer | 9 |
| nurse | 6 | bus driver | 8 |
| shop assistant | 2 | secretary | 5 |
| computer programmer | 3 | journalist | 1 |

3 Students can do this activity alone, in pairs, or in groups.
**Feedback:** whole class.

| | | | |
|---|---|---|---|
| 1 | secretary | 4 | journalist |
| 2 | nurse | 5 | teacher |
| 3 | bus driver | 6 | shop assistant |

### Teaching tip  Student-centred feedback

When students call out their answers, don't always feel you have to have the final say. Let the other students agree or disagree, and only intervene if there is clear disagreement or an answer which is incorrect.

4 Students work alone or in pairs to write sentences for the other four jobs. Monitor and offer help as necessary.

Feedback: individual students or pairs could exchange their sentences, read the descriptions, and write the job title next to each description for the writer to check. Alternatively, you could do a whole class feedback, asking individual students to read out a job description to the class. The class should then decide which job is being described.

Put the class into groups. Divide the jobs equally between the groups and ask each group to write definitions for their jobs, e.g. *A nurse is somebody who looks after sick people in hospital.*

Each group writes up their work on a piece of paper, which is then put on the wall for all students to read at the end of the activity. As the students compile their definitions, move around the class helping them with vocabulary and offering any ideas. Alternatively, the name of the job could be omitted, e.g. *This person looks after sick people in hospital.* At the end of the activity pairs walk around and discuss what they think each job is.

**5** Working alone, students listen to the dialogues and write them down word for word. To help them, put the following dialogue prompt on the board:

A   What do you do?

B

Tell them each dialogue will follow this pattern. They have to complete B's part.

Feedback: ask three students to come up to the board and write up one of the dialogues each. Other students can then assess the work to see if they agree, or if there are any mistakes. When everybody is agreed on the text of the dialogues, play them again for confirmation. Ask students to read the Tapescript on *p.107* to check their work.

1   A   What do you do?
    B   I'm a doctor.
2   A   What do you do?
    B   I work for a publishing company.
3   A   What do you do?
    B   I'm a teacher in a primary school.

**6** This is a chance for students to practise their pronunciation. Point out the example in the book to illustrate how the words are linked. Alternatively, make sure you keep the dialogues from exercise 5 on the board. Model the first example for the students and ask them where the links are. Show the links on the board, and then briefly drill the dialogue chorally and individually. In pairs, ask the students to look at the next two dialogues from exercise 5 and decide where the links are. Emphasize that they should say the sentences out loud and listen to each other in order to decide.

Feedback: call several students to the board to act as scribes. The class should tell them where to put the links. Only intervene if necessary. When all the links have been shown on the dialogues, drill briefly as above.

**7** In groups, students now consolidate their knowledge and discuss the occupations of people they know. Move around the class, checking for correct pronunciation and appropriate vocabulary. This might be a good time for you to note down any mistakes made by the students, and to go through them before moving on to the freer **Speak out** later in the unit.

# English in use

## Job adverts

**1** Students should work alone or in pairs for this exercise. This is a good chance for dictionary work (see **Teaching tip** on dictionaries on *p.28*). You can add challenge to the activity by giving a time limit of three minutes, or asking the first pair or student who finishes to shout out or raise their hand.

Feedback: ask individual students to read out their answers to the class. Let the class judge whether an answer is correct or not, only intervening if necessary (see **Teaching tip** on student-centred feedback on *p.19*).

1   If you wear good clothes, you are **smart**.
2   If you have done a job before, you are **experienced**.
3   If you speak and listen well, you have good **communication skills**.
4   If you want to do well in a job, you are **motivated**.
5   If you study at university, you get a **degree**.
6   If you earn a lot of money, you have a **high salary**.

Focus students on the box in the margin and ask the class to give you an example of an advertisement. (They should point to the job adverts on the next page.) Ask them to abbreviate the word (it is worth doing this to reinforce the tip box) and ask them where the stress goes in *advertisement* and *advert*. (The stress in *advertisement* is on the first syllable in American English.)

**2** Students can work alone, in pairs, or in groups. Change the interaction from exercise 1 to give students variety. Also remember to move students around, so that they are not always working with the same people.

Feedback: individual students can read out their answers to the class. Students should justify their answers by referring to the text.

1   five jobs are advertised (accept four as an answer if students combine waiters and waitresses as one job)
2   waiters, waitresses, bar servers   **smart / motivated**
    chefs   **experienced**
    English lecturer   **degree / experienced / good communication skills**
3   a restaurant
4   English lecturer   **three years' experience**
5   £15,885
6   by phone, e-mail, or letter

**Teaching tip  Student-centred feedback**

During the feedback, let the students ask the questions in exercise 2. You can either ask an individual to come to the front and ask the questions, or you can have different students asking questions across the class. The student asking the questions should say whether an answer is correct or not.

You can use these sections before or after the **Speak out**, or as revision prompts.

# Speak out

1 Briefly ask a few students what they do. Then get each student to write down their occupation, or refer to their sentences in exercise 1, **Vocabulary**. Remember to get students who don't have a job to write down what they would like to do.

2 Referring students to the chart, ask them to note down all the qualities and qualifications needed for their job. Demonstrate by eliciting those needed by teachers and writing them up on the board, e.g.

| qualities | qualifications |
|-----------|----------------|
| patient | a degree |
| experienced | training |
| motivated | a diploma |

3 In groups, students now tell each other about their jobs or the jobs they'd like to have, and what they entail. Move around the classroom, joining in the conversations. Help with vocabulary and pronunciation where necessary. If you have a number of students with the same job, it might be an idea to put them in the same group to see if they have similar ideas. It could make for an interesting discussion.

Feedback: ask a few students to report back to the class.

---

**Teaching tip** Error correction

Rather than focusing on grammar, you could write up words which caused problems with pronunciation on the board, and / or add good vocabulary that students have needed or used, so the students can benefit from each other's work.

---

Alternative

Instead of working in groups, you could do this as a mingling activity, asking students to conduct a class survey. Give the students a time limit of five to ten minutes to find out what other students in the class do. Encourage them to answer the question *What do you do?* in a variety of ways, and to ask each other for more information, but ask students to move on to another partner regularly so that they can speak to as many people as possible. Move around the class checking for correct pronunciation and appropriate vocabulary.

Feedback: in groups, ask students to report on two people's jobs from the class. If somebody else in the group has also spoken to that person, they should listen carefully to check that the information is correct. Alternatively, students could take it in turns to describe someone's job. The rest of the group listen to see whether they recognize or can guess the person from the description.

---

**Don't forget**

Practice exercises, Classbook, *p.83*

Teacher's Resource Pack activity 06a, *GUESS WHAT I DO*

Teacher's Resource Pack activity 06b, *JOB STRESS*

# 07
## LOVE & HATE

## Lesson aims

- Introduce and practise vocabulary for activities.
- Give students the opportunity to talk about likes and dislikes.
- Focus on the -*ing* form.

## What do you know?

> **Note**
>
> Unfamiliar vocabulary is likely to be:
> snowboarding, surfing the Net, window shopping,
> jogging, clubbing, hill-walking

1 Ask students to keep their books closed. Begin this activity by asking them what they like doing in their free time. Encourage them to ask you as well, or just tell them. Write up their ideas on the board in two columns, indoor and outdoor. See if the class can work out the difference between the two lists.

Students then work alone or in pairs to complete the activity in the book. Ask them to read through the list of activities to see if their ideas are listed and to deal with any vocabulary problems. Point out the example and remind them that some of the activities could go in either column.

| indoor | outdoor |
|---|---|
| watching TV | playing football |
| doing nothing | doing nothing |
| reading the paper | snowboarding |
| surfing the Net | reading the paper |
| going to the cinema | window shopping |
| clubbing | jogging |
| eating out | hill-walking |

### Extra

Ask the students what they think the opposite of *jogging* is. Of course there is no one answer, but different students will offer different perspectives. You might get a number of answers, ranging from *eating chips* to *sleeping*. When you first ask the question, be ready to give your ideas too, as the students might appear a little bemused at first. If the students enjoy this activity, they could continue in pairs with some of the other activities in exercise 1.

2 See if the class can come up with any more activities. They might have exhausted their vocabulary in the first exercise, so don't expect too much.

## Grammar

### Likes and dislikes

1 **Against the clock.** Give the students exactly one minute to memorize the activities in **What do you know?** Make sure they cover this section of their books when you tell them time is up.

2 Check the students understand the meaning of the coloured hearts. Demonstrate the activity, saying where you would place one or two of the activities. Working alone, students now put the activities they remember in the correct shapes in their books.

### Grammar box: Likes and dislikes

Before doing exercise 3, you could focus students on the grammar box. Elicit the language from the class by asking the students what can follow the verb *like*.

3 In pairs, students now compare their answers. Get them to count the things they have in common.

Feedback: find the most similar pair in the class.

### Extra

Ask the students what they put in the *I love* shape. Put up the different answers on the board and find out which activity is the most popular in the class.

4 Ask students to look at the -*ing* forms and to consider what the rules are.

| cook | + -*ing* |
|---|---|
| practise | remove the *e* + -*ing* |
| run | double the consonant + -*ing* |

> **Note**
>
> Students might ask you when to double the consonant. A consonant is doubled when:
> - the verb ends in one consonant
> - the final consonant has one vowel before it
> - the final syllable is stressed
>
> In British English, a final *l* is also doubled (*travelling*).
>
> You can use these verbs as further examples:
> *stop, begin, get, swim*

> **Teaching tip** Rules
>
> If students seem to be struggling, give them the three rules, and tell them to match them to the three examples. This is a useful strategy when students need help, or may understand but are finding it difficult to express themselves, or simply to save time.

5 **Against the clock.** Working alone, give the students one minute to apply the rules.

Feedback: put students into pairs to compare answers before checking as a class.

| sitting | using | trying |
|---|---|---|
| sleeping | coming | winning |

## Practice

> **Note**
>
> Unfamiliar vocabulary in the activity is likely to be:
> triathlon, flip flops, faraway, jungles

1 Students work alone to find the person who is most similar to them. Before they begin reading, go through any unfamiliar vocabulary with them.

**Feedback:** you can do a number of things here. You can ask individual students to tell the class who they are most similar to and why. With a large class, you can take a poll by asking all students who think they are most similar to Alex, for example, to put their hands up. In this way the class can see which person is the most 'universal'.

Another option is to put the students in pairs or groups to compare their ideas first. After a few minutes, you can ask individual students to tell the whole class their ideas. A poll can also be carried out, as above.

2 If you want to see how your students are coping, it might be best to ask them to work alone (see **Teaching tip** on working alone on *p.17*). As this exercise involves making inferences, you might like to go through one of the questions with the class first.

**Feedback:** whole class. Individual students can read out their answers to the class, using the text to justify their answers. Other students can agree or disagree with their ideas.

| | |
|---|---|
| cycling | Alex (triathlon) |
| pasta | Karen (Italian food) |
| pets | Alex (her dog) |
| watching videos | Colin (watching TV) |
| expensive shoes | Alex (shopping) |
| comfortable beds | Colin (staying in bed late) |
| buying Christmas presents | Alex (shopping) |
| going to the beach | Karen (swimming in the sea) |
| tropical countries | Karen (travelling) and Colin (jungles) |

---

**Teaching tip** Process language

Give your students process language to justify their answers. Here are some suggestions:
*I'm pretty sure Alex likes cycling because it says she likes the triathlon.*
*Alex probably likes cycling because the text says she likes the triathlon.*

---

3 Students listen to a variety of people expressing their likes and dislikes. As they listen, they should underline any stressed words. To practise the same sentences, put students in pairs so everybody has a chance to speak.

**Feedback:** check students' pronunciation by asking individuals to say the sentences.

See Tapescript for answers.

1   I love eating out at the weekend.
2   I can't stand doing nothing.
3   I really like watching TV in the evenings.
4   I quite like clubbing.
5   I hate reading the paper.

### Extra

Once students have underlined the stressed words, get them to use their own sentences about themselves for pronunciation practice (exercise 2, **Grammar** Likes and dislikes).

4 Tell students to read the sentences before listening, and go through any unfamiliar vocabulary (e.g. *box* = TV). Students then listen alone and try to complete the sentences. Give them the opportunity to compare answers in pairs before listening again if necessary.

**Feedback:** whole class. Play the tape / CD again to confirm students' answers.

See Tapescript for answers.

1   I love **windsurfing** ... the sea, the fresh air ...
2   Sometimes I just like **sitting** around, **doing** nothing.
3   I **can't stand** noisy pubs. I can never hear people.
4   I quite enjoy **being** alone. I don't always need company.
5   I hate **getting up** when it's still dark.
6   I quite like **watching** football on the box, but I prefer **being there**.
7   I **don't like** gardening. It hurts my back.
8   I **really hate** the weather here. It's so depressing.

### EXPAND your vocabulary

Students can use bilingual dictionaries to do this exercise in class or as homework. Remind them to copy the spidergram into their notebooks and to write example sentences for their new words.

### Extra

This vocabulary activity can be expanded in a number of ways in order to extend and practise students' new words. You could ask students to write a short paragraph which describes the activity or their own experience in some way, using the words in their spidergram. In groups, students can read each other's paragraphs and ask about each other's experiences. They can also ask for help with any new vocabulary. You may ask students to prepare a short talk rather than writing. This can then be a speaking activity, but follows the same procedure. Give students the opportunity to add their group's words to their notebooks, if they wish. This activity gives students the chance to choose their own vocabulary, talk about something they are interested in, and learn from each other.

### Can you remember ...?

You can use these sections before or after the **Speak out**, or as revision prompts.

## Speak out

1 Let students read the poem and ask you any questions. To see how much of the poem they have retained, you could write the following skeleton up on the board and ask students to come up and complete a line at a time in any order. If they don't remember the first line, they can start with another line.

I like ...

I ...

...

but

I ...

...

Alternatively you could ask the students to rewrite the poem from memory on their own, and then put them into pairs to compare.

## Alternative

You could approach the poem in a different way as a speaking activity.

### Disappearing text

Copy the complete poem onto the board or an OHT and ask students to read it out together, concentrating on the stressed words. Rub out two activities, e.g. *tennis* and *swimming*, and ask students to read it out again. Rub out the other two, e.g. *walking* and *smoking*, and ask students to read it out again. You can continue in this way, choosing key words to rub out until the board is empty or you have a skeleton like the one above. This is effectively drilling, but students usually find the memorization challenging.

2  Students now work in groups to compose their own short poem. The emphasis has changed slightly in that they must first discuss their likes and dislikes to find three things they all like and one thing nobody likes. Remind students of the possible answers to the question *Do you like ...?* given in the grammar box on *p.23*.

Move around the class as they work, joining in the conversations if you like (the students may be interested to know if you like the same things they do). Help them with any vocabulary.

3  One person from each group can now read out their poem to the class. Alternatively, put each poem up on the wall, and students can move around reading them.

**Feedback:** once students have heard or read each poem, ask them to concentrate on the differences and similarities between the poems. Is there anything everybody / nobody likes?

---

**Don't forget**

Practice exercises, Classbook, *p.85*

Teacher's Resource Pack activity 07, *LIKES AND DISLIKES*

# 08
## ZOOS & BARS

- Introduce and practise vocabulary of entertainment.
- Focus on city guides describing what's on.
- Practise describing what's on in your town.

## Vocabulary challenge

1 Begin by asking students where they go in their free time. Tell them about yourself too, by agreeing or disagreeing with their suggestions. Give your reasons, as this will prime them for exercise 4. After a short discussion, get students to look at the pictures in the exercise. Ask them what places in a town they think the pictures represent. After they have made a few suggestions, ask them to match the beginnings and endings of each place and then label the pictures. Do the first one as an example.

| | |
|---|---|
| 1 | art gallery |
| 2 | café |
| 3 | cinema |
| 4 | museum |
| 5 | bar |
| 6 | club |
| 7 | zoo |
| 8 | theatre |
| 9 | restaurant |

### Extra

With a weaker class, do a brief quiz to test the students' knowledge of places in a town or city (this will also prepare them for exercise 2). They could do this alone, in pairs, or in groups. Ask them to write down answers to the following prompts:

**This is where people go to ...**
- see films
- look at things from the past
- have a drink and a snack, or a light lunch
- look at paintings
- dance
- watch a play
- see animals
- have a drink, usually alcoholic
- have a meal

If students have worked alone, put them into pairs or groups to compare answers before the feedback session.

**Feedback:** you could make this more challenging by telling students to cover their work and call out the answers from memory. You can also give points to the first pair or group to call out a correct answer if you wish.

Draw students' attention to the box in the margin. Elicit the language from the class if you can, by asking what you can see in a cinema, theatre, and museum. This will lead naturally into exercise 2.

2 **Against the clock.** In pairs, give students three minutes to think of two things associated with each place. Encourage the use of dictionaries if necessary, and move around helping with any vocabulary difficulties. Be flexible with the time limit as the next exercise is dependent on them having sufficient vocabulary.

### Alternative

If you think your students might struggle to find relevant vocabulary, do this as a matching exercise. Write up the following pairs of words, and ask the class to match them to each place:

- exhibition / history
- film / popcorn
- coffee / cakes
- paintings / photos
- music / lights
- programme / clapping
- bears / feeding time
- cocktails / peanuts
- waiters / tablecloths

If you use this activity, you will need to adapt exercise 3. After checking answers, students can test each other in pairs.

3 In groups of four, one pair tests the other with their words.

**Feedback:** you could get each pair to read out their words to the class to see how many different words have been thought of altogether.

4 Focus students on the box in the margin and point out that we use *the* with *cinema* and *theatre*.

Point out the time phrases in exercise 4 and check understanding and pronunciation. Put an example of your own on the board. Staying in their groups, students now discuss the various places, talking about where they like going and why. Encourage them to agree or disagree with each other, as this will bring out negative language too. Monitor their discussions and collect language for an error correction slot.

## English in use
### Things to do

1 It is probably best to get students to work in pairs for this exercise, as they can divide up any words they don't know, saving time. You can also do it as a timed activity. Move around the class, helping with any difficulties.

| | |
|---|---|
| admission | is how much you pay to get in. |
| a booking fee | is money you have to pay to book tickets. |
| a matinée | is an afternoon show ... |
| subtitles | are the words at the bottom of the picture ... |
| concessions | are cheaper tickets for students, etc. |
| noon | is the same as 12.00 midday. |

**Teaching tip** Regrouping students

Rather than asking the groups to explain their words to each other as a class, you can regroup the students so that each student in the new group has different words. They can then explain their words to their new group in turn. You can organize the class as follows. First stage: students work in groups of three or four. Give each group a letter, e.g. AAA BBB CCC DDD. Second stage: regroup the students into new groups of three or four depending on the number of students in your class, e.g. ABCD. Emphasize that the students should remember their own letter for the regrouping (not you!).

2  Working alone, students now match the words and abbreviations. Alternatively, you can put up the abbreviations on the board to see how many the students know or can work out for themselves. Give them clues for those they don't know. Be prepared for any questions concerning the meaning of these words.

| Mon | Monday |
| conc | concessions |
| adm | admission |
| hols | holidays |
| perf | performance |
| mat | matinée |
| Rd | Road |
| St | Street |

3  Draw students' attention to the box in the margin. Students now skim through the *Time Out* extracts, ticking what they think they'd enjoy and putting a cross by things they'd avoid. Emphasize that the idea is not to understand every word, but simply to get a good idea of what each place is and what's going on there. It is probably a good idea to give students a time limit of five minutes to read through the extracts.

**Feedback:** hold a brief discussion to see if students have similar tastes in entertainment.

**Teaching tip** Skimming

It is important to emphasize the task when asking students to skim a text. It is a good idea to write the question on the board to focus students on what they are looking for in the text. Otherwise, they will naturally begin to read for detail. A time limit should also help to focus students' minds on the task.

**Note**

Unfamiliar vocabulary in the extracts is likely to be: Bank Hols *, subject to, senior citizens, runs
* Bank holidays are on a Monday in the UK, giving a three-day weekend. They fall on all major holidays (New Year, etc.), and once in the spring (the end of May), and the summer (the end of August).

4  This activity needs a much more detailed reading of the text (see **Teaching tip** on scanning on *p.11*). Students can use dictionaries for unfamiliar vocabulary or look to you for help.

**Feedback:** once students have checked their answers in pairs, have a class feedback session to make sure everybody is in agreement.

| A | | B | |
| --- | --- | --- | --- |
| 1 | false (*Sun 11.00 a.m.*) | 1 | false (*Wed, Thur, and Sat*) |
| 2 | true | 2 | false (*£5.00 children*) |
| 3 | true | 3 | true |
| 4 | true | 4 | false |
| 5 | *Time Regained* | 5 | 5.00–5.50 p.m. |
| 6 | the basketball match | 6 | noon |
| 7 | 020 8795 6403 | 7 | the Breakfast Club |
| 8 | £5 | 8 | 2 hours 10 minutes |

**Teaching tip** Student autonomy

You might feel it's unnecessary to have a class feedback after the students have checked their answers in pairs. Certainly, moving straight on shows the class you trust their judgement, and gives them a valuable sense of independence.

5  Students write questions for the answers using the question words in brackets, as in the example. Let them work alone here so you can check individuals' progress. Possible answers are suggested below, but students might have other variations.

**Feedback:** put students into pairs to compare their questions before checking answers as a class.

**Possible answers**
1  What's the phone number of the Natural History Museum?
2  What time does The Breakfast Club open?
3  When does the photography exhibition at the Barbican finish?
4  How much is admission for adults to the basketball game?
5  What's the phone number of the Westminster Theatre?
6  How many photographs can you see at the Magnum exhibition?

**Teaching tip** Peer support

When students are working alone, they might still feel the need to check one or two things with each other. This shouldn't be a problem. You can still get a feel for how students are coping alone. The difference between asking for advice and copying should be obvious.

## Can you remember ...?

You can use these sections before or after the **Speak out**, or as revision prompts.

## Speak out

1  If you don't come from the same place as the students, first tell them what entertainment is on offer where you live. Then ask students what cities or towns they are going to talk about. If possible, get them working in pairs or groups. Take one of the suggested places and begin an example list on the

board. Elicit daytime and evening activities. Students then complete their own lists.

**2 & 3** In pairs, students now exchange information and comment on each other's suggestions. Move around the classroom, adding your own comments to increase the interest of the discussion.

**Feedback:** ask individual students to tell the class what's on in their partner's town and what they thought sounded interesting.

## Alternative

If you have a monolingual class with students from the same town, they might not find it interesting to comment on things they are all familiar with. Instead of exercises 2 and 3, they could work in pairs and rank the list of entertainments and activities from exercise 1 according to each one's success as a tourist attraction. Pairs could then get into groups to encourage further discussion, or they could discuss their views as a class.

If time allows, and the class seems interested, students could also create their own tourist brochure outlining entertainment and activities in their town.

---

**Don't forget**

Practice exercises, Classbook, *p.86*

Teacher's Resource Pack activity 08, *A WEEKEND TRIP*

## Lesson aims

- Revise and extend vocabulary of places in a town or city.
- Practise asking where places are.
- Practise using prepositions in giving locations.

---

**Note** Giving directions

This lesson focuses on the practicalities of getting around a town, concentrating on places that students might really want to find. The language is functional, enabling students not only to ask where places are, but also to understand the reply. They should also be able to give basic directions to visitors to their own town.

---

## Speak for yourself

1 To start students thinking about the different features of a city, ask questions like *Where can you eat in a city? Where can you drink? Where do you get a bus / train? Where do you go shopping? Where do you see a film? What do you do in a park?* Then ask students to look at the map, alone or in pairs.

**Feedback:** if students have done the activity alone, give them an opportunity to compare their answers in pairs before checking as a class.

### Alternative

Copy the map onto an OHT and find the places as a class.

2 **Against the clock.** Give the students three minutes to draw a map of their own city or town. If they live in a very rural area, they might want to draw their nearest city and mark where a friend or relative lives. They can still respond to questions such as *How long does it take you to get there?*

---

**Teaching tip** Drawing

The map in the Classbook is a copy of a Japanese student's map of her town. It took her about five minutes to do. Drawing can seem like a solitary business, but it gives students time to focus on the task, consider the language they will need to communicate, and, whilst speaking, it provides them with an invaluable prop. The map itself can generate tremendous interest, as students become aware of the differences between their home area and their partner's.

With some students / groups, you may need to emphasize that the quality of the drawing is not important, and that drawing provides a useful, personal way of practising the target language.

---

3 This works best in pairs. Groups of three would also be possible. To start the activity, you could show students a map of your home town (on the board or on an OHT) so that they can ask you the questions in the Classbook. Encourage them to think of more questions.

## English in use

### Saying where things are

1 This exercise gives students the opportunity to revise vocabulary and the alphabet. They can check their alphabetical list with a partner. Any disagreements can be settled by checking the order in an English–English dictionary.

**Feedback:** ask students how many words they found. You can check pronunciation and word stress as they call each word out.

| | |
|---|---|
| bridge | roundabout |
| corner | shopping centre |
| main road | side street |
| park | traffic lights |
| pedestrian crossing | |

---

**Teaching tip** Dictionaries

Encourage students to use a good English–English dictionary appropriate to their level. The *Oxford Elementary Learner's Dictionary* has simple explanations, clear examples, and illustrations. It also has topic pages for lexical fields such as family, shapes, prepositions, and so on. One option is to provide a class set. However, if this is not possible, students should be encouraged to have their own. At this level, students will still need a bilingual dictionary, but it is important for them to feel comfortable with an English–English dictionary as soon as possible.

---

2 Students should work alone, listening to the mini-dialogues and marking the places on the map. It's a good idea to stop the tape / CD after each dialogue to give students time to mark the map.

**Feedback:** let them check with a partner, then play the tape / CD again to confirm if necessary.

| | | |
|---|---|---|
| a | 8 | supermarket |
| b | 7 | chemist's |
| c | 3 | post office |
| d | 4 | art gallery |
| e | 2 | Chinese restaurant |
| f | 1 | museum |
| g | 5 | Italian restaurant |
| h | 6 | cinema |

---

🔊1

1 A  Could you tell me where the museum is, please?
  B  Yeah, it's near the roundabout.
2 A  Is there a Chinese restaurant near here?
  B  Yes, it's on that side street, near the traffic lights.
3 A  Excuse me. Is there a post office near here?
  B  Yes, there's one just down there, between the lights and the shopping centre.
4 A  Excuse me, is the art gallery near here?
  B  Yes, it's there, on the corner.

**5** **A** Excuse me, is this the way to the Italian restaurant?
   **B** Yes, keep going, it's next to the bridge.
**6** **A** Could you tell me where the cinema is, please?
   **B** Do you know the museum? It's opposite there.
**7** **A** Excuse me, do you know if there's a chemist's near here?
   **B** Yes, there's one in that big shopping centre.
**8** **A** Is there a supermarket near here?
   **B** Yes, it's on this main road, on the left.
   **A** Sorry?
   **B** Just down here, on the left.

## Extra

It's a good idea to drill the pronunciation of the places before listening, marking the main stress on each word or phrase.

**3** Students can work together to remember which prepositions are used in the dialogues. If students are unsure about prepositions, you can refer them to the prepositions box at the bottom of the page.

**4** Check with the tape / CD.

| | | | |
|---|---|---|---|
| 1 | near | 5 | next to |
| 2 | on, near | 6 | opposite |
| 3 | between | 7 | in |
| 4 | on | 8 | on, on |

### Teaching tip   Using Tapescripts

It can be useful for students to follow the Tapescript at some stage during a listening, in order to reinforce learning. The text can be used in several ways, for example:
- as a prop for students who panic or are slower than their peers
- during feedback to clear up mysteries
- for more detailed language or pronunciation work after a listening activity
- as a model for a speaking activity

## Grammar box: Prepositions

**1** Ask students to work alone or in pairs to match the prepositions with the diagrams. This exercise aims to reinforce the language used in the previous activities, providing students with a quick reference.

| | | | |
|---|---|---|---|
| 1 | between | 4 | on |
| 2 | near | 5 | in |
| 3 | next to | 6 | opposite |

## Extra

If you have Cuisenaire rods you can use these to elicit the prepositions from the class. This gives you the opportunity to repeat any which students are unclear about, and extend the list if students already know these prepositions. If they need practice, you can give three or four rods to each pair so students can test each other. They can then do the exercise as a quick reinforcement.

**2** **Against the clock.** Give students two minutes to write their sentences. This is a simple testing device, giving students the opportunity to use the language in a practical, familiar context. You can choose whether to do this individually as a written exercise or as an oral exercise in pairs, with students taking turns to make a sentence.

**Feedback:** if students have done the exercise orally, ask different students to give one sentence with each preposition to make sure they are using them correctly.

If students have written their sentences, they can read them to a partner, whistling or 'beeping' instead of saying the preposition. Their partner should say the correct preposition. Walk around the class checking students' writing, and helping with any problems.

## Practice

**1** You can do this with the whole class. Make sure that students understand *polite*.

The polite questions are:
**B** Could you tell me where the bus station is?
**A** Excuse me, is there a post office near here?

### Teaching tip   Politeness

This exercise is to introduce students to the notion that the most direct way of asking for something is not always the most polite in English. Some people consider the British hypocritical in their politeness. However, in order not to offend, it is important that learners of the language appreciate and try to adopt the conventions. The most obvious polite words are *please*, *thank you*, *excuse me*, and *sorry*. More difficult are the replacement of *can* with *could*, *will* with *would*, and the use of *shall*. Finally, if the intonation and tone of voice is appropriate, then mistakes with the language will be less likely to offend.

**2** Students practise the intonation in polite questions.

.........................................................................

Could you tell me where the bus station is?
Excuse me, is there a post office near here?

## Useful language box

Draw students' attention to the **Useful language** box and practise the phrases. Point out the word order in the indirect questions. In exercise 3 you will probably have to help with the pronunciation of the place names.

**3** Point out that the places are all useful to know when visiting London. Put the students into pairs to practise asking polite questions. Make sure that both students in the pair get the opportunity to practise.

### Teaching tip   Recording students

Whilst doing this kind of practice, it can be helpful to record students, encouraging self- and peer-correction. If this is difficult in class, ask students to record themselves at home.

## Alternative

For further practice of the question forms, ask students to refer back to their own maps (**Speak for yourself**). Tell them to think of two or three places that they haven't mentioned on the map and write them at the bottom of the page. Students then ask each other where the places are. This gives students the opportunity to listen to real questions and give real answers.

## Can you remember ...?

You can use these sections before or after the **Speak out**, or as revision prompts.

## Speak out

1 The focus of this activity is on the kind of information tourists need in a foreign city: where to eat and where to shop. Start by looking at the map, and make sure that students can pronounce the names of the streets correctly – this will help them when they do the pair work activity. (You could also ask them which countries the cities are in – Memphis and Washington, the USA; Montreal and Vancouver, Canada; Auckland and Christchurch, New Zealand; Brisbane and Canberra, Australia.)

2 Students work in pairs. Student A looks at the map on *p.105* and B looks at the map on *p.106*. Make sure that the task is clear. Each student has six places marked on their map, and six places to find. A and B ask each other where the places they need to find are, and mark them in the blank labels on their maps.

It's probably best if A and B alternate, rather than A asking all six questions, followed by B. Encourage students to use different questions – there are three suggestions given for them on *p.105* and *p.106*.

Make sure that students sit opposite each other and give clear instructions rather than pointing to the maps. They can exchange maps at the end to find out how successful their directions were. Monitor the conversations, but try not to get involved. You can note errors in language and intonation for feedback later.

---

**Don't forget**

Practice exercises, Classbook, *p.87*

Teacher's Resource Pack activity 09, *LOST IN THE SUPERMARKET*

# 10
## GOOD & BAD

### Lesson aims

- Extend and practise a range of adjectives for *good* and *bad*.
- Focus on film reviews.
- Practise giving opinions.
- Practise using *quite*, *really*, and *absolutely* with adjectives.

## Listening challenge

1 Draw students' attention to the adverts and elicit what they are for.

| | |
|---|---|
| *By the River* | a film |
| Oriente de Cuba | a concert |
| *China Green* | a novel |
| John Blake retrospective | an exhibition |
| Pizzeria la Quercia | a restaurant |

You can ask students how much time they devote to these forms of entertainment in an average week or month. Ask questions like *How often do you go to the cinema? Do you often visit art galleries? Which do you spend most money on? Do you like reading? When and what do you read? Which of these things do you enjoy most? Which do you never do?*

2 Play the tape / CD twice. On the first listening, ask students to identify which place or event the six speakers are talking about. They can number the adverts in the order they hear them referred to. When they listen again, they should try to note down the words that gave them the answers. You can also ask them to put a tick or a cross next to the corresponding advert, depending on whether the opinion was positive or negative. A strong class will come up with some of the modifiers in exercise 1, **Vocabulary**.

1 It was **really good** (✓). I **read** it in a week. (*China Green*)
2 I thought it was **disappointing** (✗). I usually like **thrillers**, but this was **boring**. And **three hours** was much too long. (*By the River*)
3 Well, the **food** was **really good** (✓), but it cost over £40, which is a lot. (Pizzeria La Quercia)
4 It was **nothing special** (✗) – the café was better than the **paintings**! (John Blake retrospective)
5 I thought it was **awful** (✗) – I gave up on **page 20**. (*China Green*)
6 It was **absolutely fantastic** (✓) – I love **Cuban music**. (Oriente de Cuba)

1 It was really good. I read it in a week.
2 I thought it was disappointing. I usually like thrillers, but this was boring. And three hours was much too long.
3 The food was really good, but it cost over £40, which is a lot.
4 It was nothing special – the café was better than the paintings!
5 I thought it was awful – I gave up on page 20.
6 It was absolutely fantastic – I love Cuban music.

## Vocabulary

### Opinion adjectives

> **Note** *Good* and *bad*
>
> It's useful for students to be able to express their opinions in a variety of ways. *Good*, *bad*, and *nice* are quite limiting. By exposing students to authentic reviews (which include strong adjectives and common modifiers), it should encourage them to feel that they can use authentic entertainment guides in real life. Not only that, but they will be able to express their own views with greater confidence and a good range of vocabulary.

1 Students should be familiar with the idea of star rating, which is used to rate many things from restaurants to films and novels. Five stars signify the best and one star the worst.

**Feedback:** you could put the chart on the board. This will be useful for exercises 2 and 3.

| | |
|---|---|
| terrible | * |
| nothing special | ** |
| not bad | *** |
| really good | **** |
| brilliant | ***** |

2 **Against the clock.** Give students three minutes to add the words and phrases to the chart, alone or in pairs. Dictionaries should be English–English where possible. If students are using dictionaries, it's a good idea for them to mark the word stress at the same time. This will help with exercise 3.

**Feedback:** ask different students to come up to the board and add the adjectives and phrases to the correct column as other students call them out.

| | |
|---|---|
| * | awful |
| ** | disappointing, not very good |
| *** | OK |
| **** | very good |
| ***** | great, fantastic, excellent |

> **Teaching tip** Using dictionaries to check pronunciation
>
> If your students are not familiar with using dictionaries for checking pronunciation and word stress, it's a good idea to look at an example with them. Copy a word with the phonetic symbols and word stress symbols onto the board, e.g. *disappointing* /ˌdɪsəˈpɔɪntɪŋ/. Point out that the stress symbols used in dictionaries may be different from those you use in class. Emphasize that an understanding of these symbols enables students to check pronunciation independently.

3 Use the tape / CD or yourself to model the words and phrases. In pairs or as a class, ask students to decide how many syllables the words or phrases have and which syllables are stressed. Mark their ideas onto the words on the board. Then ask students to repeat the complete sentences or phrases as a class after you or

the tape / CD. Focus on intonation as well as word and sentence stress, pointing out how much can be inferred from the speaker's tone of voice.

# English in use

## Giving your opinion

1  You can do this activity directly in groups of three (A, B, and C), or put students into A groups, B groups, and C groups to discuss their answers first before getting into A, B, C groups. Tell students to copy the table into their notebooks. Encourage students to write complete phrases rather than just single words when they note the positive and negative adjectives.

You could refer students to the tip box in the margin below the texts which explains the wording of the reviews.

| Adam | **likes** Pierce Brosnan as Bond and the scene where he jumps out of the window in Bilbao. |
|------|------|
| | **dislikes** Robert Carlyle as the bad guy. |
| | *+ good, excellent, the best, terrific, exciting* |
| | *– a bit disappointing* |
| Natalie | **likes** Pierce Brosnan and Sophie Marceau, and the scene where they are skiing in the mountains. |
| | **dislikes** nothing (but doesn't usually like Bond films). |
| | *+ quite good, better (than I expected), really like, brilliant* |
| | *– terrible* |
| James | **likes** Bond movies and the chase with the speed boat. |
| | **dislikes** Bond killing a woman, and some of the action scenes aren't very exciting. |
| | *+ really cool* |
| | *– not as exciting, quite shocking, nothing special* |

2  In A, B, C groups, students complete their tables by asking questions as in the example. Encourage students to help each other with spelling, rather than looking back at the text.

3  This can be a discussion in the same groups or with the whole class. Students should give reasons for the star rating. *I think Adam gives it four stars. He says it's excellent entertainment, but that Robert Carlyle is disappointing.*

| Possible answers | |
|------|------|
| Adam | **** |
| Natalie | *** |
| James | ** |

## Useful language box

Try to elicit the modifiers from the class, giving the first letter of each one as shown in the book. Emphasize the idea that the three modifiers *quite*, *really*, and *very* can be used with simple adjectives such as *good*, *bad*, and *nice* to change their strength. *Really* and *very* are stronger than *quite*.

Strong opinions (very positive or very negative) are often emphasized by using *absolutely*. The one-star or five-star idea should be a good way to make the concept stick in students' minds.

## Practice

1  Individually, students listen and note down the adjectives and modifiers. You may want to stop the tape / CD after each one.

See Tapescript for answers.

| 1 | A | What did you think of the book? |
|---|---|---|
| | B | It was **really good**. |
| 2 | A | How was the film? |
| | B | I thought it was **disappointing**. |
| 3 | A | What was the restaurant like last night? |
| | B | Well, the food was **really good** ... |
| 4 | A | How was that exhibition you went to? |
| | B | It was **nothing special**. |
| 5 | A | How was the book? |
| | B | I thought it was **awful** ... |
| 6 | A | What was the concert like? |
| | B | It was **absolutely fantastic**. |

2  Ask the students to mark the main stresses and listen to the intonation before repeating the sentences after you or the tape / CD. Alternatively, or subsequently, students can practise in pairs.

See Tapescript for answers.

1  It was really good.
2  I thought it was disappointing.
3  The food was really good ...
4  It was nothing special.
5  I thought it was awful ...
6  It was absolutely fantastic.

3  Let students do this alone or as a class.
   **Feedback:** write the three possible questions on the board as a reference for exercise 4. Give students the opportunity to practise saying the questions.

| What did you think of it? |
|---|
| How was it? |
| What was it like? |

4  If you feel it's necessary, demonstrate the first dialogue (or a similar one) with a confident student, or ask two students to demonstrate it for the class. Then ask pairs to continue with the next two dialogues.

Possible dialogues

A I went to that new club last night.

B Oh, how was it?

A It was absolutely awful. The décor was cheap and the music was terrible.

A I went to an art exhibition yesterday.

B What was it like?

A Not very good. The paintings were OK, but the photos were nothing special.

A We went to that new café this morning.

B What did you think of it?

A It was excellent. The building is beautiful and the coffee is fantastic.

---

**Teaching tip** Functional dialogues

It's often a good idea to get students to memorize short functional dialogues. To do this, get all the students to practise the same dialogue with a partner. At this point they use the prompts to help them. Then swap the pairs and, without their books, they practise the dialogues again. If you want to make it more challenging, they can do two dialogues, once as A and once as B, and then swap round. Alternatively, you can memorize the dialogues by using the disappearing text technique, as shown in the **Alternative** activity on *p.24*.

5 This gives students an opportunity to practise talking about their own experiences and opinions, before going on to the **Speak out** section.

**Feedback:** monitor this activity closely, picking out good phrases that students have used, and a few errors for comment, too.

## Alternative

If you want to make this activity more structured, ask students to write prompts for dialogues as in exercise 4. Elicit the question *What did you do last week?* from the students before they question each other about their activities and opinions in pairs or groups.

## Can you remember …?

You can use these sections before or after the **Speak out**, or as revision prompts.

# Speak out

1 To make this clear, it's probably best to demonstrate it yourself. From the list in the book (famous actor, film, singer or musician, and sports personality) choose two you like and two you dislike and write one name on each of four large pieces of card for everyone to see. Students then do the same.

2 Use one of your own cards as an example. Hold it up and give your opinion of the person or film on the card. Then refer students to the tip box in the margin, and invite students to join in with their comments. Keep reminding students to use language from the lesson. Monitor the discussions, but try not to get involved unless you feel the discussions need a boost. Note errors for later.

**Feedback:** did students find that they generally agreed or disagreed with each other? Add your own comments if you want to.

---

**Don't forget**

Practice exercises, Classbook *p.89*

Teacher's Resource Pack activity 10, *WHAT DO YOU THINK?*

# 11
## OUT & ABOUT

## Lesson aims

- Practise using the present continuous for talking about plans.
- Focus on spelling -ing forms.
- Give students the opportunity to talk about plans.

**Note** Present continuous

Although the present continuous is traditionally introduced to students to describe what you are doing now, it is actually much more commonly used to talk about future plans. We focus on its use to describe what you are doing **now** in lesson 13, in the context of mobile phones.

## Speak for yourself

1 Focus students' attention on the chart, and brainstorm weekend activities. Demonstrate by telling students about your own favourite time. Then ask students to choose their own favourite time individually and write a sentence about it.

2 Group discussion.

**Feedback:** ask a spokesperson from each group to tell the class what the favourite time of the weekend is for the majority of the group, and what the most common weekend activities are.

3 Do this with the whole class. Ask how often people do something different at the weekend. Help with vocabulary, writing new words and phrases on the board.

## Grammar
### Present continuous for plans

1 Explain that there are two different dialogues about two couples' plans for the weekend. Ask the students to look at the pictures and elicit the subject of each of the dialogues – one is about going to an Italian restaurant and the other is about going away. Ask students to underline words in each section of the dialogue that refer to either going away or eating out. Suggest using different coloured pens to make this clearer. Students then work in groups to sort out the two dialogues.

### Alternative

You can write key vocabulary on the board under the headings **going away** and **eating out**.

| going away | eating out |
|---|---|
| We're going to Paris! | ... going out for dinner ... |
| a special offer ... | That Italian place, Umberto's. |
| When are you leaving? | The food's really excellent. |
| We're getting the train ... | |
| accommodation | |
| staying | |

2 Students listen and confirm their ideas. Be prepared to stop the tape / CD after each A / B exchange to allow students to check.

See Tapescript for answers.

**Conversation 1**
A What are you doing this weekend?
B Oh, nothing much. Shopping, maybe, and a bit of telly.
A Well, if you feel like it, Bella and I are going out for dinner on Saturday, and you'd be more than welcome to come.
B That sounds great – where are you going?
A That Italian place, Umberto's. The food's really excellent. We're meeting Keith there about 8.00. Do you know where it is?
B No, I don't actually.
A Well, we're driving so we can pick you up. About 7.45?
B OK. See you then.

**Conversation 2**
A What are you doing this weekend?
B We're going to Paris! Jane saw a special offer, £69 all in, so we thought let's go for it.
A Fantastic! When are you leaving?
B We're getting the train on Friday evening, at 7.30.
A And is everything included? Accommodation and everything?
B Yeah, but we're not staying anywhere nice, I don't think. But anything's OK for £69!
A Absolutely. Well, have a great time. And we'll see you on Monday.
B OK. See you then.

3 This exercise focuses on the use of the present continuous for asking and talking about plans. Students can work alone, and then check in pairs.

**Feedback:** when they have finished, tell students to refer back to the dialogues to check. It may be clearer for them to refer to the Tapescript on *p.107*.

1 What **are you doing** this weekend?
2 Bella and I **are going out** for dinner on Saturday.
3 We**'re meeting** Keith there at 8.00.
4 We**'re driving** so we can pick you up.
5 We**'re not staying** anywhere very nice.

### Extra

To focus on some of the useful vocabulary from the dialogues, you can mix up the following pairs of phrases and do a matching exercise:

| | |
|---|---|
| nothing much | not a lot |
| a bit of | some |
| if you feel like it | if you want to |
| you'd be more than welcome to | we want you to |
| we can pick you up | we can take you in our car |
| a special offer | a good price |
| let's go for it | let's do it |
| is everything included? | is it all in the price? |

Alternatively, ask the students to pick out what they think are useful phrases and then find other ways of saying the same thing.

## Grammar box: Present continuous

**Note**

The second conversation presents *we're not* as the negative form, and the Present continuous box presents *we / you / they aren't*. Point out to students that these are the same.

The grammar box gives all the forms of the present continuous. Focus students on the example sentences, which represent the spelling rules for the *-ing* form. If you have done lesson 07 with your class, elicit the rules from the class, or if they find this hard, put the rules (below) on the board and ask them to match them to the verbs in the examples.

> Verbs ending in a consonant preceded by another consonant or a double vowel, add *-ing*.
>
> Verbs ending in *-e*, drop the *-e* and add *-ing*.
>
> Short verbs ending in a consonant preceded by a single stressed vowel, double the final letter and add *-ing*.

Ask students to apply the rules to the verbs in the language box in the margin.

Emphasize the word order in questions by getting students to underline the questions in the dialogues. Focus on pronunciation of the questions, asking students where the strong and weak forms are, then briefly drilling them as a class.

**Present continuous box**
What are you doing this weekend?
When are you leaving?
Where are you going?
**Margin box**
swimming   leaving   looking

## Practice

1 Students do this alone and check with a partner.

1 I'm meeting Mary for a coffee.
2 I'm going to a Chinese restaurant with some friends.
3 Staying in and watching TV.
4 Nothing special.
5 I'm going down to London for the day.
6 I'm spending a couple of days with my parents.

2 Tell the students to listen and check their answers with the tape / CD.

**● 2**

1 I'm meeting Mary for a coffee.
2 I'm going to a Chinese restaurant with some friends.
3 Staying in and watching TV.
4 Nothing special.
5 I'm going down to London for the day.
6 I'm spending a couple of days with my parents.

**Feedback:** ask different students to read out the sentences for you to put on the board. Alternatively, ask different students to come up to the board and write the sentences as other students call them out. This is a good idea for confirming word order, and is useful for exercise 3.

3 Ask students to predict the questions for the answers on the board. They could do this in pairs.

4 You can write up students' ideas on the board and ask the class to judge which questions are the most likely. Students compare their ideas with the tape / CD. Make sure you give credit to possible answers even if

they are different from the tape / CD. After checking, students practise the same questions in pairs, giving their own answers. Remind them to concentrate on pronunciation.

See Tapescript for answers.
The answer that can go with any question is *Nothing special*.

**● 3**

1 A   What are you doing after this lesson?
  B   I'm meeting Mary for a coffee.
2 A   What are you doing for dinner tonight?
  B   I'm going to a Chinese restaurant with some friends.
3 A   What are you doing this evening?
  B   Staying in and watching TV.
4 A   What are you doing tomorrow evening?
  B   Nothing special.
5 A   What are you doing on Saturday?
  B   I'm going down to London for the day.
6 A   What are you doing this weekend?
  B   I'm spending a couple of days with my parents.

**Teaching tip**  Writing up students' ideas

In this kind of exercise it is a good idea to tell students that you are going to write exactly what they say on the board (even if it is not correct). Give the class the opportunity to correct the sentences if they wish, but don't interfere. Simply act as a scribe. This prevents students depending on your judgement and tends to focus them more clearly when they come to listen.

### Can you remember ...?

You can use these sections before or after the **Speak out**, or as revision prompts.

## Speak out

**Teaching tip**  Memorizing

This activity works best if students don't refer to their books all the time. Consequently, give students enough time to memorize their plans so that they can talk freely to each other without being hampered by books or bits of paper.

1 Make sure students understand the vocabulary. Demonstrate by putting your own plans on the board.

**Teaching tip**  Personalizing activities

Encourage students to think about their weekend and put down activities that they really are planning to do. If they are not going to do those activities shown in the book, tell them to add things they are going to do or might like to do. This will make the activity more real and much more enjoyable.

2 Students mingle until they find someone whose weekend plans most resemble their own.

3 Encourage students to ask as many questions as they can so that they make the plans as real as possible.

### Alternative

As they mingle, the students don't have to wait until all their plans are the same as somebody else's. They can organize to do different things with different people, e.g. they can plan to spend the morning with one partner and the evening with another. With a bigger or stronger class, you may even want students to plan an activity together in groups.

4   This is optional and serves to wrap up the **Speak out**.
    Partners join with other pairs to form groups.
    Students tell each other their plans, while the other
    pair asks questions. However, you may feel that the
    activity has run long enough, particularly if the
    students have done the **Alternative** suggested above.
    In that case, you can ask one or two general questions
    to finish, e.g. *Do many people have the same plans as you?*
    *Is it difficult to agree? Do you like doing things alone, with*
    *one other person, or in a group?*

**Don't forget**

Practice exercises, Classbook, *p.90*

Teacher's Resource Pack activity 11a, *TIME PHRASES*

Teacher's Resource Pack activity 11b, *MAKING PLANS*

## Lesson aims

- Introduce and practise transport vocabulary.
- Practise making enquiries about public transport.
- Focus on public transport announcements.

## Vocabulary challenge

1 To introduce the topic, you can ask students how they like to get around. Is there any form of transport they avoid? Why? A few general questions will also prime them for the next exercise. Then focus students on the pictures and the acrostic. They can complete it alone, in pairs, or in groups.

| | | | |
|---|---|---|---|
| 1 | taxi | 6 | plane |
| 2 | underground | 7 | coach |
| 3 | car | 8 | ferry |
| 4 | train | 9 | motorbike |
| 5 | bus | | |

2 Working alone, tell students to mark the sentences with a tick or cross, depending on whether they are true or false. If your home town is different from the students', demonstrate by telling students about taxis where you come from.

3 In pairs, students compare ideas. Multilingual groups will have more to talk about here. Students from the same town might be better off in larger groups to see if they all have the same opinions. Alternatively, conduct a quick class survey to see if everybody agrees, e.g. *Do you think taxis are cheap?*

### EXPAND your vocabulary

Focus students on the **Expand your vocabulary** box. In groups, you could give students a time limit to brainstorm groups of words for *plane* and *bus*. Add challenge by seeing which group can think of the most words. Encourage students to use dictionaries to check meaning and spelling. Remind them to add their words to their vocabulary books and write example sentences.

**Possible answers**

**plane** check-in desk, check in (v.), gate, departure lounge, take off, land (v.)

**bus** conductor, driver, bus stop, fare, double-decker, get on, get off

### Alternative

You could divide the class into two teams. (Split the teams up into smaller groups if you have a big class.) Ask Team A to brainstorm words for *plane* and Team B to brainstorm words for *bus*. Then put students into pairs to share their words. They should teach each other any unfamiliar words.

## English in use

### Using public transport

1 Students listen to the five dialogues and match them to the pictures. Depending on the level of your class, you might like to do the first one with the class as an example.

**Feedback:** put students into pairs to check answers together before class feedback, or go straight to class feedback. Ask students what gave them the answer in the dialogues. This will prepare them for the following exercise.

| | |
|---|---|
| 1 | a |
| 2 | c |
| 3 | b |
| 4 | e |
| 5 | d |

🔊1

1 A Could you stop here, please?
  B Sure.
  A How much is that?
  B £5.40, please.
  A Here you are. Keep the change. And could I have a receipt, please?
2 A Excuse me. Is this the train to Glasgow?
  B Yeah, it is.
  A What time does it get there?
  B 6.33.
3 A Can I help you?
  B Yes, I want to go to Dublin this weekend. What's the best way to get there?
  A Well, there are lots of cheap flights at the moment, in fact we've got a special offer …
4 A The city centre, please.
  B That's 75p.
  A Sorry, how much did you say?
  B 75.
5 A A return to London, please.
  B That's £27.50. It'll be £16.00 if you can wait till 9.00.
  A It's OK, I need to travel now.
  B OK, that's £27.50 then, please.

### Alternative

If you feel your students' listening skills are weak, put the following five lines on the board:

Could you stop here, please?
A return to London, please.
Can I help you?
Is this the train to Glasgow?
The city centre, please.

Before they listen, ask them to match the lines to the five pictures. Also, get them to identify the speakers in the pictures. Doing this will also give them a hand with the following exercise.

2 Continuing to work alone, students now complete the gapped sentences. Playing each dialogue twice should be enough, but repeat them if the students ask you to. If you like, students can also work in pairs from the start, so they can help each other.

**Feedback:** if students have been working alone, they can check in pairs before class feedback, or you can discuss the answers as a class. Ask individual students to read out their answers. Let the rest of the class decide if answers are acceptable or not.

> 1 Could you **stop here**, please?
>   How **much is that**?
>   Keep the **change**. And **could I have** a receipt, please?
> 2 Is this **the train to** Glasgow?
>   What time does it **get there**?
> 3 What's **the best way** to get there?
> 4 Sorry, **how much** did you say?
> 5 A **return** to London, please.

**3** Students choose their four words from each dialogue and practise the dialogues in pairs. Allow them to refer back to the Tapescript if they need help.

### Alternative

Ask students to work in groups of three. After choosing their words, they take turns to practise the dialogues in pairs. The third student looks at the Tapescript and should decide if a dialogue has been said correctly or not, and should also act as a prompt if anybody is having difficulty remembering the dialogues. The more the class is encouraged to be independent, the better.

## Useful questions box

Working in groups, pairs, or alone, focus students on the **Useful questions** box. Let them read through the questions, so they can ask you about any unfamiliar words. Alternatively, ask them to use dictionaries whilst doing the exercise.

Now ask students which questions could be asked *during* a journey (they may suggest different possibilities from those below). You could also ask them what *kind* of journey.

> **Possible answers**
> 2 taxi, also possibly while buying a ticket on a bus or train
> 5 any kind of journey
> 6 any kind of journey
> 9 bus, train, or plane
> 10 taxi

Draw students' attention to the box in the margin. Ask the students to continue each question in an appropriate way, referring them to the **Useful language** box if they are having difficulties. Working alone, ask students to write their own questions for each one. You could introduce students to the use of *take* with *How long ...?* e.g. *How long does it take to get to ...?*

> *How long ...?* is for asking about time.
> *How far ...?* is for asking about distance.

---

**Teaching tip**  Real questions

Encourage students to ask real questions, e.g. *How far is it from your house to school? How long is the flight from Japan to England?* Help where necessary. Then ask students to work in pairs to ask and answer their questions.

---

## Practice

> **Note**
> Unfamiliar vocabulary is likely to be:
> change (v.), it depends, direct, just after

**1** Ask students to match the answers to the questions in the **Useful questions** box. Point out the example before they begin. Students shouldn't have too many problems with vocabulary in these exercises, but you could ask them to read the sentences quickly to check before they do the exercise.

| | | | | | | | |
|---|---|---|---|---|---|---|---|
| a | 3 | d | 7 | g | 2 | j | 11 |
| b | 6 | e | 10 | h | 5 | k | 9 |
| c | 1 | f | 4 | i | 8 | l | 12 |

**2** Students listen to check their ideas. Play the dialogues one by one, asking the students to tell you which words are stressed, and briefly drilling the questions.

🔊2

> a  A  Is the flight direct?
>    B  No, you have to change in Singapore.
> b  A  How long is the journey?
>    B  Two and a half hours.
> c  A  What's the best way to get there?
>    B  Probably by taxi.
> d  A  Is it better to fly or go by train?
>    B  It depends – flying's much faster.
> e  A  Could you stop here, please?
>    B  Yes, sure.
> f  A  Do I need to change?
>    B  No, it's direct.
> g  A  How much is that?
>    B  £27.50.
> h  A  How far is it?
>    B  About 50 miles.
> i  A  Where does the bus leave from?
>    B  The central bus station.
> j  A  Is this the bus for London?
>    B  No, you want the blue one over there.
> k  A  What time do we get there?
>    B  Just after 11.00.
> l  A  How often do the buses go to the city centre?
>    B  Every ten minutes or so.

**3** In pairs, ask students to practise the dialogues. Move around the class, checking to see if they are saying them correctly.

**4** **Against the clock.** Give students two minutes to make the questions. Ask them to work in pairs as this will encourage them to say the questions out loud. Give them extra time if necessary.

**Feedback:** whole class.

> 1 Which platform is the train to London leaving from?
> 2 How late is the train from London?
> 3 Which gate is the flight to Newcastle boarding at?
> 4 Where do British Airways flights leave from?
> 5 When does it arrive?

---

> **Note**
> Students may want to begin the questions with the preposition, e.g. *From which platform is the train to London leaving?* This is theoretically correct, but can sound formal or stilted – reassure them that it is more natural to have the preposition at the end of the question.

5 Students now listen for the missing information. Point out that what they have in their books is only a summary of the words on the tape / CD. Emphasize that they should only listen for the necessary information, e.g. platform number. If they are having difficulties, tell them to call out *Stop* when they hear the relevant information. Give students the opportunity to read the announcements before listening, and make sure they realize that they provide the answers to the questions in exercise 4.

1 The train to London is leaving from platform **five**, not platform **seven**.
2 The train from London's King's Cross is **35** minutes late, and is now arriving at 17.15.
3 Flight BA 1462 to Newcastle is now boarding at gate **A34**.
4 All British Airways flights leave from terminal **four**.
5 The flight takes 55 minutes, and arrives at **2.30** local time.

1 This is a platform alteration. Would all passengers waiting on platform 7 for the 10.30 to Paddington please go to platform 5? Platform 5 for the 10.30 to Paddington.
2 GNER apologizes for the late arrival of the 12.15 from London King's Cross. It is currently 35 minutes behind schedule and is due to arrive at 17.15.
3 Flight BA1462 to Newcastle is now boarding at gate A34. Gate A34 for BA1462 to Newcastle.
4 All Qantas and British Airways flights leave from terminal four.
5 ... and we'll be coming round with drinks and a light snack. Our flight time today is about 55 minutes, so we should be arriving at around 2.30 local time.

## Can you remember ...?

You can use these sections before or after the **Speak out**, or as revision prompts.

# Speak out

1 Demonstrate by eliciting three cities in your own country or a country you know well. Tell students to ask you questions about travelling between them using the prompts in the book.

If you have a multilingual group, ask students to think about their own countries. You can group students according to nationality for this stage, or ask students to work alone. Then mix up nationalities for the group work in the next activity to create an information gap.

If your group is monolingual, encourage them to think of a foreign country they know quite well. Again, you can group them according to countries, splitting them up for exercise 2 to create the same information gap.

Alternatively, with a monolingual group, ask students to think of three cities in their own country, but from the point of view of a tourist visiting their country. In exercise 2, other students will have the chance to improve on or agree with suggestions.

2 In groups, students now exchange information and comment on each other's suggestions. Move around the classroom, adding your own comments to increase the interest of the discussion. Monitor for good language and any problems.

**Feedback:** ask individual students to tell the class what they have learnt from another student. You could put examples of good language and errors on the board and ask students to correct the errors, or leave this to another lesson.

## Alternative

If students have approached the activity from the point of view of a tourist visiting their country, you could add interest to exercise 2 by doing it as a roleplay. In pairs, Student A takes on the role of someone local to the city, and Student B is a tourist. They should perform their dialogues and then swap roles. Monitor and collect language for a feedback session.

### Teaching tip  Feedback

In feedback sessions after pair work or group speaking activities, it is a good idea to ask students to report back on their partner's ideas, rather than repeating their own information. When a class gets used to this strategy they will automatically concentrate on what their partner is saying, but with a new class it might be a good idea to tell them what you are going to do before they begin speaking. This will ensure that they listen carefully to what their partner is saying.

### Don't forget

Practice exercises, Classbook, *p.91*

Teacher's Resource Pack activity 12, *GETTING TO HEATHROW*

# 13
## HERE & NOW

## Lesson aims

- Practise using the present continuous to talk about now.
- Focus on the present continuous and the present simple.
- Give students the opportunity to write e-mails.

## What do you know?

> **Note**
> Unfamiliar vocabulary in the text is likely to be:
> book (v.), I'm pretty sick of it

1  Students work in pairs to find the mistakes. Tell them there are sixteen mistakes and point out the scoring categories. It may be a good idea to give them a time limit of five minutes. With a stronger class you could ask students to use a marking code like the one outlined in the **Teaching tip** on peer correction on *p.49*.

> Hi! Thanks **for** (1) the e-mail. I **am sitting** (2) **in** (3) the **computer** (4) room of Hopeman College. We can book the PCs **here** (5) to send e-mails. **It's** (6) lunchtime, so I have a few **minutes** (7) …
> At the moment **we're** (8) working hard for our English **exam** (9) – it's **difficult** (10). I **am** (11) still working for Pizza Rapide as a **waiter** (12), but I'm pretty sick **of** (13) it. Spiros and I **are** (14) **looking** (15) for other **jobs** (16).
> How's your dog?

2  Working in groups, students share ideas to see if they can find more of the mistakes. If any students think they have already found sixteen, put them in a group where only a few mistakes have been found.

3  Go through the mistakes with the class.

   **Feedback:** encourage students to write out the correct version in their notebooks. This will be useful for exercise 5 on *p.41*.

> **Teaching tip**  Error correction
> Copy the text with the mistakes onto the board or an OHT. You can then ask individual students to come up and correct them.

## Grammar
### Present continuous

> **Note**
> Unfamiliar vocabulary is likely to be:
> view, loads of, on our way home, flat tyre

1  You could give students a time limit of two minutes to read the four extracts and match them to the pictures. To prepare them for the task, discuss the pictures first, asking students what they can see in each one.

   **Feedback:** whole class.

### 1 c  2 d  3 a  4 b

### Extra

Test the students' memories of the pictures. After doing the exercise, ask groups to close their books and write as many sentences about the pictures as they can. Give them a time limit of two to three minutes.

Ask a group to come and write **one** of their sentences on the board. If the sentence is relevant, they start with ten points.

Now other groups can challenge the correctness of the language in the sentence. If they challenge correctly, they get two bonus points, while the group who wrote the sentence loses two points, i.e. they now have eight points. If they challenge wrongly, they lose two points, i.e. they now have minus two points. Groups can challenge as much as they like.

At the end of the challenging, if there are still mistakes, correct them yourself and deduct a further two points, i.e. the group who wrote the sentence now have six points.

Now ask a new group to write a sentence, and so on. All sentences must be original, i.e. not on the same topic as previous sentences. Thus the group with the most original sentences has a distinct advantage. Continue until there are no more sentences.

2  Ask students to read the sentences again and underline all the examples of the present continuous. Ask the class if these examples refer to now or the future.

> 1  it's snowing
> 2  I'm sitting
> 3  I'm taking
> 4  we're waiting
> All of the above examples refer to *now*.

To highlight the difference, write up sentences on the board that refer to the future, for example:

I'm meeting my mum **tomorrow** for a coffee.

We're having dinner together **tonight**.

John's coming round **this afternoon**.

They're going to Bali **next year**.

Ask the class if these sentences refer to now or the future, and ask students how they know.

### Alternative

With a strong class, after discussing the sentences in exercise 2, write four sentences on the board in the present continuous. Two should refer to the present and two to the future. Ask students in pairs to discuss which sentences are about the present and which are about the future. Ask them to highlight which words gave them the answer. For example:

I'm meeting Susan for a drink **tomorrow evening**.
I'm reading an absolutely fantastic book **at the moment**.
**Be quiet!** I'm watching television.
I'm so happy. I'm going on holiday **next week**.

You could also point out the difference between the two sentences referring to the present. Ask students which sentence refers to this exact moment, and which one refers to now generally (these days). This point is reinforced in the **Present continuous for now** box.

## Grammar box: Present continuous for now

To confirm the use of the tense, focus students on the grammar box. Draw students' attention to the two sentences in the present simple by way of contrast. Alternatively, you could write the four sentences on the board and ask the class how they know whether the sentences are present simple or continuous. They should point out the verb forms and the key words. Focus attention on the two different uses of the present continuous (*now* or *these days*). If students need reminding of the form of the present continuous, refer them to *p.35* in lesson 11.

> I'm going into the supermarket now.
> I'm having driving lessons at the moment.
> I go to the supermarket every day.
> I usually have a driving lesson on Thursdays.

## Practice

1 Students listen to the three messages on answering machines left by callers with mobile phones.

2 Students work in pairs to complete the gaps.

> See Tapescript for answers.

........................................................

a *You have one message. Please wait.*
Hi, it's me. I'm on the train. We're just **leaving** the station, and it's still **raining**. The train's really busy tonight, but at least it's not late, so I should be home soon. I'm having a burger right now, so don't worry about dinner. **Love** you.
b *You have no old messages and one new message.*
Hi, it's Michael. I'm having a couple of beers in the pub with John, so I'll **be** home a little late. **Keep** the dinner warm! Bye.
c *You have one new message.*
Hi, just me. We're on our way back now. Mary wants to pop into the supermarket first. Just what I need ... my feet **are killing** me. Can you **get** in a pizza? Thanks. Bye.

3 Play the recording again for students to check the answers.

> Verbs in the present continuous are:
> a We're (just) leaving ...
> ... it's (still) raining.
> I'm having ...
> b I'm having ...
> c ... are killing ...

---

**Teaching tip** Listening

Allow the students to operate the tape recorder / CD player themselves. Choose a confident student to do this, or suggest different students take over for each message. They can repeat the messages as often as they like (as they could on an answering machine). This makes the listening more realistic and gives the class more control.

---

4 This is a good opportunity to see whether students have grasped the use of the present continuous as opposed to the present simple. You may want students to work alone at first, in order to see if anyone is having problems. Do the first one together and refer them to the grammar box if they have doubts.

**Feedback:** ask students to compare their answers in pairs, before checking as a class.

> 1 I usually **get** lots of e-mails.
> 2 I'm walking the dog. I'll be home soon.
> 3 I'm in the bank. I'm cashing some cheques.
> 4 On weekdays we get up at 7.00.
> 5 Postmen do a lot of walking.
> 6 A Where's Jack?
>    B He's fixing the light.

5 Here, the emphasis is on writing, using Vladimir's e-mail (the corrected version!) as a model. Students can either use the cartoons in the book as prompts, or write about their own lives. You could ask the class if they write e-mails, how often, and who to.

Before the students begin, see how much they remember of the original e-mail (the corrected version) without looking at the text. You can do this orally, in pairs or as a class. Then go through the prompts with the class, asking different students the questions, e.g. *Where are you now? What are you doing? What is the weather like? Where are you living? Who are you living with? Do you like your current situation? Are you doing anything to change things?*

It is worth spending time on this preparation stage, as it will make the writing activity easier for students. Remind students to decide who they are writing to. If they wish to write to someone in the class, they can give them their e-mail to read when it has been checked.

**Feedback:** you can correct students' texts as they are writing, but you may wish to collect their work for one final check.

### Alternative

Ask one or two students who do not mind having their work on display to write out their e-mail on an OHT. They or you can then correct it in class, asking the rest of the students to help.

---

**Teaching tip** Authentic communication

If students have access to an e-mail facility (either at school or home), you can make this activity much more authentic and enjoyable by telling them to write to someone they know (a friend, penfriend, or relative) in English. If they can't do this for any reason, tell them to write to someone in the class or school, and failing that, to you. They can prepare their e-mail in the class and, when they are happy with it, send it to whoever they have chosen to write to. This can help bring the real world into the classroom.

---

### Alternative

Working alone, get students to think of their present situation in some detail using the prompts as a guide. Students can invent a different situation for themselves if they prefer. Once they have had time to consider things, put them in pairs to question each other. They can then write sentences describing their partner's situation, to consolidate their work.

### Can you remember ...?

You can use these sections before or after the **Speak out**, or as revision prompts.

# Speak out

This is a board game for students, testing their knowledge of the present continuous. Go through the rules to check the students know what they are doing. Point out that if students land on a square that has already been talked about, they have to give a new reason for what is happening in the picture. As they play, move around listening to students' answers. Only intervene if a group seems unable to judge if something is correct or not. Below are suggested answers for what's happening in each picture – students will think of their own ideas for why.

**Feedback:** when the class have finished playing, go through the possible answers in the key and elicit any alternatives.

**Possible answers**

1 She's looking at her watch ... she's tired / she's late for school / the dentist.
2 He's reading a newspaper ... he wants to know the football results.
3 He's sleeping under a tree ... he's tired.
4 She's crying ... she's upset.
5 The dog's running ... it's playing a game / it's dinner time.
6 She's examining a patient ... he isn't feeling well.
7 He's waiting for a train ... he's going to work.
8 He's looking out to sea ... he's thinking about when he was young / waiting for a ferry.
9 She's talking on the phone ... she's ordering a pizza.
10 She's looking over a gate / waiting ... her father / mother is coming home soon.
11 They're waiting in a queue ... they're waiting for a bus / waiting to buy tickets.
12 He's going into a bank ... he works there / he's getting some money.
13 She's looking at the sky ... she's looking at a bird / a plane.
14 He's sitting on a park bench ... he's having a rest / waiting for a friend.
15 He's talking on a walkie-talkie ... he's calling for help.
16 He's cooking ... he's making dinner for his family.
17 He's packing a rucksack ... he's going camping / on holiday round the world.
18 It's sitting on a windowsill / looking out of a window ... it's waiting for its owner / watching a bird.
19 They're looking at rings ... they're getting engaged / married.
20 He's closing his shop ... it's 5.30 / he's going for lunch.

**Teaching tip** Giving time limits

If your class have a tendency to keep games going for as long as possible, impose a time limit. Then if a group hasn't finished, the winner is simply the person furthest along the board.

**Don't forget**

Practice exercises, Classbook, *p.92*

Teacher's Resource Pack activity 13, *WHAT'S HAPPENING?*

## Lesson aims

- Talk about how you keep in touch.
- Focus on contact details.
- Give students the opportunity to take and leave phone messages.
- Practise saying phone numbers.

## Speak for yourself

1 **Against the clock.** Give students five minutes to write sentences about themselves. Before they begin, go through the example with them and use this to draw attention to the tip box in the margin. It may be a good idea to revise adverbs of frequency briefly. You can also demonstrate by telling them about yourself, e.g. *I hardly ever write letters*. Make sure they put a cross on each line to establish how often they do each thing. Be prepared to supply them with any extra vocabulary they might need.

2 Working in groups, students discuss their ideas and compare their habits.

   Feedback: ask different students to compare themselves to the rest of their group. You can then monitor how well they have been listening to each other.

## Vocabulary
### Contact details

1 Students match the descriptions with the different parts of the business card. Check understanding by questioning students who work for companies, e.g. *What's the address? What's your job title? What's your e-mail address?*

| | | | |
|---|---|---|---|
| 1 | company name | 6 | telephone number |
| 2 | job title | 7 | fax number |
| 3 | address | 8 | e-mail address |
| 4 | zip code | 9 | web site |
| 5 | area code | | |

### Alternative

Bring in a variety of business cards and hand them out. You can elicit the different parts of a business card by asking students what information is on the cards. They can then compare their ideas with the business card in the book.

2 Draw students' attention to the tip boxes in the margin on extension numbers and how to say phone numbers. You could write a phone number on the board to elicit the language from the class, e.g. *01223 640233*. If you feel the class needs to practise saying phone numbers before doing the exercise, put up more phone numbers on the board and ask students to read them in pairs or to the class.

   Put students into A / B pairs and refer them to *p.105* and *p.106* in the Classbook. Emphasize that they have different information missing on their cards and should find the missing information by asking their partner appropriate questions, as in the example.

### Teaching tip  Phone numbers

This is a good opportunity to draw attention to intonation and pausing when dictating phone numbers. Dictate a few numbers to the students, then ask them to repeat the numbers back to you, copying your intonation and pauses. Also emphasize that they should give the complete number for their partner to write down, rather than stopping to wait for their partner to catch up. However, point out that they can repeat the number as often as necessary.

3 In pairs or groups, students now ask each other for their phone numbers.

   Feedback: make sure each pair or group has a spokesperson to report back to the class. You can then create a class phone directory on the board for everybody to copy.

### Teaching tip  Board scribes

Remember to use the students as board scribes. This gives them more practice in listening. It also gives multilingual classes a chance to get more used to each other's different accents.

### Alternative

You could expand this activity by telling students to ask each other for more information related to work. If most of your students work, they could ask and answer about the information given on business cards, e.g. *What's your job title? What's your fax number?* If they don't work, you could hand out real business cards to all the students (see **Alternative**, **Vocabulary**, exercise 1), and tell students to assume that person's identity. Alternatively, they could create their own business cards for their ideal job. Then do a mingling exercise, telling students to imagine they are at a business conference. Teach them *networking* = getting to know people who may be useful for you at work.

## English in use
### Taking and leaving messages

1 Draw students' attention to the pictures of Michael and Julia and ask questions about them to build up a context for the phone call. Point out that Michael is the caller and that Julia is taking a message. Then ask the students to read the text in their books so that they know what information they should be listening for.

   Feedback: put students into pairs to compare their ideas before playing the tape / CD again if necessary.

**Michael** phoned. Can you call him back on **224 6785** before **9.00** tonight or **8.30** tomorrow morning? It's about **the meeting tomorrow**.

| Julia | Hello? |
|---|---|
| Michael | Hello? **Is that** Julia? |
| Julia | Yes, **speaking**. |
| Michael | It's Michael **here**. Is Robert **there**? |
| Julia | No, **sorry**. He's at the gym. Can I **take** a message? |
| Michael | Yes, **please**. It's **about** the meeting tomorrow. Can he **phone me** back before 9.00 tonight? I'm going out then. |
| Julia | OK, just let **me get** a pen. Right ... he's to phone you back before 8.00. |
| Michael | No, before 9.00. I'll be in till 9.00. |
| Julia | Sorry, before 9.00. What number can he **call you** on? |
| Michael | 224 6785. |
| Julia | 224 6785. Fine. |
| Michael | If he can't do that, I'll be at home until 8.30 tomorrow morning. |
| Julia | OK. Before 9.00 tonight or 8.30 tomorrow morning. |
| Michael | Great. Thanks, Julia. Bye. |
| Julia | OK. Bye. |

2  Ask students to turn to the Tapescript on *p.108* to check their ideas and listen again.

**Feedback:** go through any problems with the class.

## Useful language box

In pairs, or alone, ask students to try to complete the gaps in the phone call from memory. If students have worked alone, give them an opportunity to compare their ideas in pairs before going through it as a class.

**Feedback:** it is a good idea to go through the phone call with the class, asking different students to give each statement or response. In this way you can check pronunciation and briefly drill any phrases which are causing problems. Finally, students can check with the Tapescript if they still have any doubts.

See Tapescript for answers.

## Practice

1  **Against the clock.** In pairs, give students three minutes to find the other eleven mistakes in the phone conversation and correct them.

**Feedback:** ask how many mistakes the students have found.

2  Tell the students to listen to the conversation and check their ideas. Tell them to highlight any mistakes they didn't find as they listen, and then to correct the mistakes after listening.

**Feedback:** tell students to refer to the Tapescript on *p.108* to check quickly, or if you prefer, show the version with mistakes on an OHT and ask the students to call out the mistakes and corrections for you to mark.

See Tapescript for answers.

| Deirdre | Hello (1)? |
|---|---|
| Jim | Hello, is **that** (2) Deirdre? |
| Deirdre | Yes, **speaking** (3). |
| Jim | **It's** (4) Jim. Is George **there** (5)? |
| Deirdre | No, I'm sorry. He's at the library. Can I **take** (6) a message? |
| Jim | Yes, please. It's **about** (7) our meeting tomorrow. Can he **phone me** (8) back before 7.00 this evening? I'm going out then. |
| Deirdre | OK, just let me **get** (9) a pen. Right ... before 7.00. What number can he **get** (10) you on? |
| Jim | 334 6885. |
| Deirdre | That's 334 6885. Fine. |
| Jim | Great. Thanks, Deirdre. **Bye** (11). |
| Deirdre | OK. **Bye** (12). |

3  This activity allows the students to apply what they have done so far. Ask them to read the message and ask questions to check understanding, e.g. *Who phoned? What's her phone number? What's it about? Who do you think Rachel phoned?* Then ask students to write the telephone dialogue for the message. You could do the first two lines on the board with the class and then ask them to continue. Elicit a name for the receiver.

**Feedback:** go round checking students' writing and helping with vocabulary or problems. Encourage the students to use the two conversations in the book as models.

Ask students to practise their dialogues. If they find this easy, suggest they cover their dialogues and practise the conversation from memory.

4  Put students into groups and ask pairs to perform their dialogues for each other. Ask students to sit back to back to make the conversation more realistic. Encourage them not to look at their dialogues, but let them refer to the message as a prompt. Ask one listener to note down any differences between their dialogues, and the second listener to give the speakers a mark out of ten for their performance.

**Feedback:** give the groups time to discuss the differences and marks. Tell students they should justify their mark, but keep this light-hearted.

**Can you remember ...?**

You can use these sections before or after the **Speak out**, or as revision prompts.

## Speak out

1  Divide the class into As and Bs. Give the students a few minutes to prepare their part of the dialogue orally with a partner (As working together and Bs working together). Encourage them to practise useful phrases from the lesson. Walk around, checking understanding of their roles and helping with vocabulary and pronunciation.

Draw attention to the box in the margin, or elicit the questions before pointing the box out.

2  Ask students to sit back to back in A / B pairs. Remind Student B to have a pen and paper handy for taking the message. Monitor and make a list of any problems and good points for comment after the activity.

**Feedback:** tell pairs to compare their messages in groups.

3  Ask students to change partners and roles. Make sure they close their books before practising the conversation again.

**Don't forget**

Practice exercises, Classbook, *p.93*

Teacher's Resource Pack activity 14a, *TELEPHONING*

Teacher's Resource Pack activity 14b, *TALK TIME*

# 15
## UPS & DOWNS

## Lesson aims

- Introduce and practise different ways of saying *How are you?*
- Revise and extend vocabulary of feelings.
- Practise giving advice.

## Listening challenge

### Note

Students tend to learn the standard *How are you? Fine, thanks*. The **Listening challenge** is designed to introduce students to different but very common ways of starting a conversation. It also emphasizes the use of intonation to convey mood.

1 Students listen to the tape / CD and note down the different ways of starting a conversation, before checking with a partner.

   **Feedback:** write the variations on the board, draw attention to the elision between *How* and *are*, and drill the questions briefly.

See Tapescript for answers.

| | |
|---|---|
| 1 | How are you doing? |
| 2 | How's life? |
| 3 | How are things? |
| 4 | How are you? |
| 5 | How's it going? |

### Teaching tip  Drilling fast speech

Encourage students to copy and exaggerate intonation and examples of fast speech after you or a tape / CD. It is often more fun and snappier if they copy you. Emphasize that they do not have to speak like this, but that it is important to recognize fast speech because this is what they will hear. Drilling of this sort should be a fun challenge.

2 Students listen to the complete dialogues and decide how the friends feel (tone of voice is as important as what they say). They should write the number of each dialogue under the correct part of the scale. Encourage the students to describe the feelings represented in any way that they can, e.g. *very happy, happy, OK, sad, very sad*.

| | | |
|---|---|---|
| 1 | A | How are you doing? |
| | B | Not so bad, thanks. |
| 2 | A | How's life? |
| | B | Great! |
| 3 | A | How are things? |
| | B | Not so good, really. |
| 4 | A | How are you? |
| | B | Fine, thanks. |
| 5 | A | How's it going? |
| | B | Could be better. |

| | | | |
|---|---|---|---|
| 1 | happy (4) | 4 | OK (3) |
| 2 | very happy (5) | 5 | sad (2) |
| 3 | very sad (1) | | |

(The number in brackets refers to the number on the scale.)

3 Students practise the dialogues, copying the intonation on the tape / CD. You may want to play the tape / CD one dialogue at a time and drill the students before they try it in pairs. Monitor this part of the activity quite closely.

4 This is a mingling activity. Encourage students to ask and answer each other in a variety of ways and to use body language, too, e.g. smile, shake hands, or wave. It may become quite loud, but it won't last long and is a good warmer for the beginning of the lesson.

### Teaching tip  Mingling

Where possible, ask students to move desks and chairs to create a space in the middle of the room before a mingling activity. It makes the room feel less restricted and means that students can walk about freely.

## Vocabulary

### Feelings

### Note

This is not a complete list of adjectives to describe feelings, so encourage students to add any more that they know. The list has more negative than positive words as we tend to give advice (see **English in use**) to people who are feeling bad.

1 **Against the clock.** In pairs, give students three minutes to put the words into the correct column. Once they have done the words they know, suggest they divide the remaining ones between them and look them up in an English–English dictionary. Tell the students to focus on the example sentences for each word. These will immediately indicate whether the feeling is good or bad.

| feeling good | feeling bad |
|---|---|
| excited | worried |
| relaxed | nervous |
| happy | bored |
| | fed up |
| | tired |
| | stressed |
| | angry |
| | upset |

2 Ask students to add their own words.

   **Feedback:** you can write their words on the board, checking spelling and pronunciation.

**3** Ask students to work alone and then compare in pairs or as a class. Encourage students to think how they would feel in the situations and to put the appropriate adjectives. There may be some discussion about the answers depending on individual points of view.

**Feedback:** ask students questions about how they would feel, e.g. *How do you feel when you've got an exam? How do you feel when you're going on holiday?*

| Possible answers | | |
|---|---|---|
| 1 nervous / worried | 4 | tired / bored |
| 2 excited / happy | 5 | bored |
| 3 fed up / angry | 6 | upset |

### Extra

You could extend this activity by telling students to ask each other, *What do you do when you're nervous / bored / worried ...?* They could do this in pairs, reporting back on their partner's more unusual habits. Alternatively, they could mingle and try to find someone in the class who does the same things they do.

Refer students to the tip box in the margin and ask them to underline examples of the three different ways of talking about your feelings in exercise 3.

**4** Students listen to the different sounds or words and note the feelings that they experience after each one. They may find that they don't know the right words in English. If so, they can write down the feeling in their own language first and check it in a bilingual dictionary before the feedback.

**Feedback:** students can compare their feelings with a partner or in a larger group.

1 *The sea.*
2 Thank you for waiting.
3 *A dog whimpering.*
4 *At the dentist* – Open wide ... wider.
5 *Classical music.*
6 You have exactly three hours. The exam starts now.
7 Will you marry me?

### Alternative

Arrange the students in a circle, with just a notebook and pen on their laps. Proceed as above, although you might suggest that students close their eyes while listening.

For monolingual groups, students can use each other as a resource for unknown words, using the question, *How do you say _____ in English?* Otherwise, students can use dictionaries. You can then note new words on the board with a quick example.

The advantage of the circle is that it can create a more relaxed atmosphere for the feedback as students can talk to each other across the circle about their feelings. Where appropriate you can extend the discussion by asking, *Are there other times when you feel angry, happy, nervous ...?*

## English in use

### Giving advice

**1** Students can work alone or in pairs and brainstorm adjectives to describe how the people in colour are feeling. Suggest that they may want to use more than one word.

| Possible answers | | |
|---|---|---|
| a nervous, worried, upset | c | fed-up, angry |
| b tired, stressed, worried | d | happy, excited |

**2** Ask students to match the conversations they hear to the pictures. They may have written different words to the ones on the tape / CD. This doesn't matter as long as they have a good reason. Unless it's a particularly strong class, play the tape / CD twice. Before they listen for the second time, ask students to listen for two ways of asking, *What's the problem?*

**Feedback:** whole class. Draw attention to the box in the margin by asking students if they heard the two other ways to say *What's the problem?* in the listening.

| | |
|---|---|
| dialogue 1 (*fed up* – problems with his computer) | c |
| dialogue 2 (*nervous, not very well* – she's got an exam) | a |
| dialogue 3 (*stressed, tired* – working late) | b |
| dialogue 4 (*excited, very happy* – she's getting married) | d |

*What's the problem? = What's wrong?* and *What's the matter?*

1 A Are you all right? You look a bit fed up.
  B Yes, I am.
  A What's wrong?
  B I'm trying to send an important e-mail and my computer keeps crashing.
2 A You don't look very happy. What's the matter?
  B Oh, I've got an exam today and I'm so nervous. I really don't feel very well.
3 A How are you?
  B Fine, thanks.
  A You don't look fine. You look worried.
  B Well, yeah, I'm a bit stressed about work right now and I get very tired working so late.
4 A Wow! *You* look excited!
  B Mm! I am. Feeling *very* happy, in fact!
  A Well, come on. Tell me!
  B Jake's asked me to marry him!

**3** This exercise introduces *should* and *shouldn't*. The dialogue is the same as in conversation 3 of the previous exercise, except that the friend goes on to give advice. Students can predict the advice before listening and completing the sentences.

| See Tapescript for answers. |
|---|

A How are you?
B Fine, thanks.
A You don't look fine. You look worried.
B Well, yeah, I'm a bit stressed about work right now and I get very tired working so late.
A I think it's crazy. You **should talk** to your boss about how you feel, and you **shouldn't work** so many hours. You've got a life to live!

### Useful language box

The box follows on directly from exercise 3 and serves to consolidate the use of *should*. Students write their own examples to help them remember the structure and to give them something to refer to in future. As it is a reference, it's important that their examples should be correct. Give students the opportunity to compare their sentences in pairs.

4  It's a good idea to brainstorm different advice onto
   the board and practise it briefly as a class before
   students work in pairs and decide on their own
   advice. This will emphasize the pattern of *should /
   shouldn't* + infinitive.

5  Students practise the conversation and advice in the
   same pairs.

6  Ask the class to listen and compare the advice on the
   tape / CD with their advice. Ask *Do you agree with her
   friend's advice? Why / why not? Do you think your advice is
   better?*

A   You don't look very happy. What's the matter?
B   Oh, I've got an exam today and I'm so nervous. I really don't feel
    very well.
A   Maybe you should take some aspirin and go to bed for an hour.

## Can you remember ...?

You can use these sections before or after the **Speak out**, or
as revision prompts.

# Speak out

**Teaching tip**  Sensitivity

Make sure that students understand that they will be
talking about the statements they mark as true. This
gives them the opportunity to filter out any that they
would prefer not to discuss. For example, the statement
*I never have enough money* could be sensitive for some,
and students should not feel pressurized to talk about
their problems. Equally, they should add a problem of
their own at the bottom of the list only if they wish to
talk about it with another student.

1  Help students with any unfamiliar words here.

2  Students have the opportunity to practise expressing
   feelings and giving advice. Demonstrate the activity,
   encouraging the students to ask you questions in
   order to find out more about the problem. For
   example:

**You**  I can't give up smoking.

**Students**  How much do you smoke? When do you smoke
most? Do you smoke with friends or alone? Why do you
smoke? Why do you want to give up smoking?

**You**  I never get a holiday.

**Students**  What's your job? How many hours do you work?
Why do you think you never get a holiday? Is there someone
who can do your job for a week?

It's a good idea to put some example questions on the
board, or question prompts to remind the students to
ask different questions, e.g.

*How much / many? Why? When? What? How often?*

## Alternative

Put students into four groups and give each group about nine
strips of paper. Ask each group to choose three problems
from the questionnaire and to brainstorm three pieces of
advice for each. Students then write their ideas on different
strips of paper. On the back of each piece of advice, they write
the problem. For example:

**Problem**  I hate going to the dentist.

**Advice 1**  Relax.

**Advice 2**  Think about something else.

**Advice 3**  Don't eat sweets.

Shuffle the strips and then put them all onto a central table,
problem-side up. In pairs, students then find out about each
other's problems. If they need help for ideas on what advice
to give, they can consult (but not remove) the ideas on the
table. Before they give the advice, they must think about the
grammar and insert *should* or *shouldn't*. You may want to
demonstrate this with a student first.

**Don't forget**

Practice exercises, Classbook, *p.94*

Teacher's Resource Pack activity 15, *WHAT'S IT LIKE
STUDYING IN BRITAIN?*

## Lesson aims

- Revise and extend food and cooking vocabulary.
- Focus on understanding menus.
- Study and practise using countable and uncountable nouns.
- Give students the opportunity to talk about food and dishes they like.

## Speak for yourself

### Note

Food is a topic that involves and interests most people. It is an excellent way for students to learn more about each other's culture. The answers to the **Speak for yourself** section will reflect a combination of cultural and individual preferences and is therefore relevant to all classes, whether multilingual or monolingual.

1  This exercise should be done individually. However, if students need help with vocabulary, encourage them to use each other as a resource, rather than you. If it is difficult to explain something, it is often easier to draw it. Remind students to copy the spidergram into their vocabulary books.

### Extra

Bring in pictures of the food mentioned in exercise 1 (or any other food that you think will help with the lesson) and have a quick quiz. Divide the class into two teams and tell them to stand in front of the board. Divide the board into two halves as well. Give Player 1 in each team a pen. Hold the first food picture up with another piece of card covering it. Slowly uncover the picture by sliding the piece of card down the front of it. As soon as Player 1 in either team recognizes what the food is, they run to the board and write down its name. You can decide whether to allow team members to help (by whispering, otherwise they would be telling the other team as well), or not. A point is scored only when the word is right and spelt correctly. Continue until all the pictures are finished.

2  Students add another item of food or drink to each box. They then work in pairs or small groups to compare their ideas.

**Feedback:** you can show the class your own version of the spidergram (on the board or pre-prepared on OHT) and ask students to comment on how similar or different your eating habits are to theirs. This will interest students as it tells them something about you and, if you come from a different country, will give them some insight into your culture. You can then ask students about themselves and each other, e.g. *Do you and your partner / group eat the same things at the same time? How are you the same / different? Did you find out anything surprising?*

## Vocabulary

### Food and menus

### Note

The menu here has a mixture of British standards and some more international meals. Although students may already know some of the basic vocabulary of the food on offer, it is unlikely that they will know all the food, or the different words for how the food can be prepared. These activities aim to make reading a menu less daunting.

1  Make sure that students know what *vegetarian* means. Focus students on the food itself in this exercise, not the adjectives. Ask them to label all the food words, e.g. V for vegetable, M for meat, and F for fish. In this way they can easily identify the meals that are suitable for vegetarians. Students can work in pairs and use each other or a dictionary for any unfamiliar food words.

**Feedback:** check understanding of the vocabulary in these dishes.

> **vegetarian dishes**
> pasta with tomato and fresh basil sauce
> baked potato with cheese
> baked potato with baked beans
> **for vegetarians who eat fish**
> grilled salmon with steamed courgettes
> fried haddock and chips
> tuna mayonnaise

2  Ask students to underline the adjectives in the menu and complete the table alone.

| adjectives | verb | food |
| --- | --- | --- |
| baked | to bake | potato, beans |
| grilled | to grill | salmon |
| steamed | to steam | courgettes |
| roast | to roast | beef, potato |
| fried | to fry | haddock, rice |
| boiled | to boil | rice |

### Teaching tip  Classroom management

When students are working alone, stronger students who finish earlier can be asked to form groups to check their answers together. Alternatively, they can be paired up with a weaker student to help.

3  Students could work in pairs for this exercise. Different countries will prepare food in different ways, so in a multilingual class students may find each other's ideas interesting.

| verb | possible answers |
|---|---|
| to bake | fish, bread, cakes |
| to grill | steaks, sausages |
| to steam | fish, vegetables |
| to roast | chicken, pork |
| to fry | eggs, bacon |
| to boil | potatoes, cabbage |

Refer students to the tip box in the margin. Elicit different ways of preparing potatoes.

## Extra

You may want to have a supply of labelled food pictures or a wall chart of food to help students explain their ideas. Use these to confirm what students want to say and to help with vocabulary if they are still having problems.

4 Ask students to look at the chart in exercise 2 to find the difference between the adjectives and verbs.

The adjectives all end in -ed except for roast.

5 This is a pronunciation exercise to practise vowel sounds and diphthongs. The important thing is to show how words that are spelt differently can sound the same. The students' own words do not have to be connected with cooking.

| A | B | C possible answers |
|---|---|---|
| grill | bill | hill, fill, ill |
| fry | pie | try, fly, cry, high |
| bake | steak | cake, shake, make |
| roast | toast | coast, most |
| steam | cream | team, seem |

6 Ask students to write sentences about their food preferences. Emphasize that they must include adjectives from exercise 2. Demonstrate by telling them about your own preferences. When they are ready ask them to work in pairs to discuss their preferences. Monitor for pronunciation.

# Grammar

## Countable and uncountable nouns

**Note**

Countable and uncountable nouns are not restricted to food, and this is taken into account in **Practice**, *p.95*.

The grammar box focuses on *There are some / There's some* and *There are no / There's no*. This is easier to learn than *There isn't / aren't any*, but if you feel it is appropriate, and certainly if students have come across it, you may want to point out the options.

1 By thinking about the food they have in their own fridge, students personalize the activity. They should try to list a variety of food. You may want to help with vocabulary or let them use dictionaries.

## Alternative

Before doing exercise 2, divide the board into two columns (one for countable and the other for uncountable nouns).

Ask students to call out some of the things in their fridge. Put the words into the columns yourself and after a few examples ask students what the columns mean. Continue by asking students to put the words in the right column themselves.

2 Students work alone, referring to the language in the grammar box to write sentences about the food in their fridge. They should then give their sentences to a partner to correct.

### Teaching tip Peer correction

When correcting each other's work, it is a good idea for students to use the code that many teachers use. This involves indicating a mistake with a symbol and giving the students the opportunity to correct their own mistakes. A simple code might be as follows:

Sp = spelling
Gr = grammar
T = tense
Vo = vocabulary
W.O. = word order
∧ = word missing
/ = not necessary

You should be on hand to check that the students have correctly indicated their partner's mistakes or to help with disagreements. Even if they are not always right, it is important that students are encouraged to check their work carefully and accept suggestions from people other than the teacher.

## Practice

1 Ask students to work alone at first to check if they have understood the concept of countable and uncountable.

**Feedback:** give students the opportunity to compare in pairs before going through the exercise with the class.

1 Have you got any brown bread?
2 Do you want some spaghetti?
3 There are no apples. (There aren't any apples.)
4 How much coffee shall I buy?
5 How many sandwiches are there for lunch?
6 Can you buy some fruit?

## Extra

For further practice, students work in pairs to write their own exercise for another pair. They can write five sentences and include three or four mistakes. This is a challenge that makes students really think about the language.

2 **Against the clock.** Give students three minutes to write a shopping list of the ten most common things the average household in their country buys. These will differ from country to country, e.g. in Greece nearly every household buys tinned milk, square white bread for making toasted cheese sandwiches, olive oil, and feta cheese for making salads. In Britain, most households buy a breakfast cereal of some sort, fresh milk, and instant coffee.

3 Ask students to compare their lists in pairs and speculate about different countries.

**Feedback:** you can draw up a list of items common to all countries and those that are unique to certain countries. In a monolingual class, it is interesting to see whether everybody comes up with the same list. If not, you can get the class to negotiate a national top ten.

## EXPAND your vocabulary

Elicit the opposites of the examples *expensive* and *open*. It's a good idea to ask students to work in pairs to find the 'opposites' of the words. This is not straightforward, and you may wish to do it as a class after giving pairs a few minutes to think about it. They will have ideas, but not necessarily the correct vocabulary. Remind students to copy the words into their vocabulary books.

| | |
|---|---|
| delicious | disgusting / horrible |
| red wine | white wine |
| black coffee | white coffee |
| sparkling mineral water | still mineral water |
| strong coffee | weak coffee |

## Can you remember ...?

You can use these sections before or after the **Speak out**, or as revision prompts.

## Speak out

1 Give students time to prepare what they want to say, looking back through the lesson for vocabulary. You may want to describe a favourite meal of your own to start with. You could encourage students to draw things if they want to; many students enjoy this and often draw utensils, etc. Be on hand to help with vocabulary.

2 Students get into groups to talk about their favourite dishes. In multilingual classes try to put students with different nationalities together. In monolingual classes try to create a good mix of male / female and different ages. Even if students know the dishes that others are describing, the point is to talk about them in English and make sure that they convey their message. Encourage students to ask each other questions. It may be a good idea to put some on the board, e.g. *Why do you like it? How do you eat it? Is it expensive? Is it traditional in your country?* Monitor for pronunciation problems and collect examples of new / useful vocabulary used by students.

   **Feedback:** ask general questions, e.g. *Which dishes would you most like to try? Which is the most unusual? Which is the most expensive? Which dish is the most difficult / easiest to make? Why? Which dishes can you also find in your country?*

---

**Don't forget**

Practice exercises, Classbook, *p.94*

Teacher's Resource Pack activity 16, *WHAT DO YOU EAT?*

---

## Lesson aims

- Focus on restaurant guides and abbreviations.
- Practise booking a table.
- Practise describing restaurants.

## Speak for yourself

1 Ask students to look at the pictures and decide what type of eating out each one represents. Encourage them to give a personal response to the pictures.

**Feedback:** ask for general reactions, e.g. where they would / would never eat.

2 Tell students to read and think about the questions before working with a partner. Alternatively, they can ask you the questions first to help prepare them for the activity. Encourage students to think of more questions if they can. Try not to spend too long on this section, as there may be some overlap with **Speak out** at the end of the lesson.

**Feedback:** you can do this as a class survey. Draw columns on the board and elicit different types of restaurants students eat at across the top. Put ticks in each column on the board to see which is the most popular way of eating out. You can then ask the class questions, e.g. *Why do you think x is popular? Do you think your parents / grandparents / children like the same restaurants as you? Do you eat in different places for different occasions?*

### Alternative

The pictures represent a variety of eating out styles. If you feel that they are not representative of the styles your students may be used to, you can provide other pictures of your own.

## English in use

### Understanding restaurant guides

### Note

The texts in this section are from a real restaurant guide, and have only been very slightly modified. They still include language that students will find challenging. The point of the activity is to show students that they can use an authentic guide effectively without understanding every word. Don't go through every unfamiliar word unless it hinders comprehension.

1 In pairs, ask students to think of at least one typical dish or type of food for each kind of restaurant.

**Feedback:** whole class. If students are interested and are having problems with spelling, make a list of the different types of food they suggest on the board under each type of restaurant.

Possible answers
see **Alternative**

### Alternative

Only do this if you think students have very little idea about different types of restaurant. Write a selection of the following types of food on the board for the students to match to the restaurant types. They can add another one or two of their own.

| | |
|---|---|
| Far-Eastern | sushi, raw fish, noodles, rice |
| coffee shops | coffee, tea, pastries, cakes |
| Chinese | sweet and sour chicken, spare ribs, spring rolls |
| burgers and steaks | hamburgers, chips / fries, steaks |
| vegetarian | salads, vegetable soup |
| Italian | pasta, pizza |

2 Students match the descriptions of the restaurants to the headings on *p.52*. Tell them to underline the words that gave them the answers. They can do this alone at first, or in pairs, but make sure they compare their ideas in pairs.

**The Best Far-Eastern Restaurants**
Daruma-Ya (*Japanese*)
**The Best Coffee Shops**
Café Florentin (*café, croissants, tarts, caffeine*)
**The Best Chinese Restaurants**
Oriental Dining Centre (*dim sum and noodle bar*)
**The Best Restaurants for Burgers and Steaks**
The Rock (*steak / burger and chips*)
**The Best Vegetarian Restaurants**
Isabel's (*vegn*)
**The Best Italian Restaurants**
Caprice (*pizzas*)

3 Students identify the remaining restaurant and suggest a heading.

Phenecia
The Best Mediterranean Restaurants
The Best Spanish / North African Restaurants

4 Write the word *abbreviation* on the board and *abbr* beside it, and check understanding. Draw attention to the tip box in the margin and the abbreviations and price key in the restaurant descriptions.

expensive   exp

Write the words from the exercise on the board and ask students to cover the texts and guess what the abbreviations are. They should then check in the texts. Highlighter pens are useful here.

| | |
|---|---|
| smoking | smk (Isabel's) |
| near | nr (Phenecia) |
| vegetarian | vegn (Phenecia, Isabel's) |
| very | v (Isabel's) |
| possible | poss (Phenecia) |
| Thursday | Thu (Caprice) |
| last orders | LO (Daruma-Ya, Caprice, Phenecia) |
| closed | cl (Daruma-Ya) |

**5  Against the clock.** Give students three minutes to answer the questions. Although you are timing them, you can ask the students to call out when they have finished. The first to finish can then call out their answers and the rest of the class agree or disagree.

| | | | |
|---|---|---|---|
| 1 | Café Florentin | 5 | Oriental Dining Centre |
| 2 | 662 4014 | 6 | Isabel's |
| 3 | 10.30 p.m. | 7 | per person |
| 4 | Sunday | 8 | £40–£60 |

**6**  In pairs, students make up their own questions. Check them before they give them to another pair to answer.

## Alternative

Pass round a sheet of paper for students to write their questions on, so that you can have a class quiz. Give students two minutes to read all the texts again. Divide the class into teams (about four students per team) and tell them to close their books. Call out the questions. Correct answers get two points, with one for a bonus. This activity is good for listening and reinforces the language of the section.

If you notice that one team is getting all the answers, you can go round the class more systematically asking questions. This is inevitably slower and less snappy.

## Booking a table

**1**  Students could listen first and then complete the dialogue, or predict the missing words before listening and checking their answers with the tape / CD.

**▶1**

| | |
|---|---|
| Waiter | Hello, Caprice. |
| Customer | Hello, I'd like to **book** a table, please. |
| Waiter | Certainly, when **for**? |
| Customer | This evening, about 8.30. |
| Waiter | **How many** people? |
| Customer | Six. |
| Waiter | Right, let's have a look. Yes, that's fine. And the **name** is? |
| Customer | Lambeth, **that's** L-A-M-B-E-T-H. |
| Waiter | Thanks, and could I just **take a phone number**? |
| Customer | Yes, **it's** 554 2888. |
| Waiter | Great. See you at 8.30, Mr Lambeth. |

**2**  Tell the students to check their answers with the Tapescript on *p.109*. Ask for any possible alternatives.

See Tapescript for answers.
**Possible alternatives:**

| | |
|---|---|
| book | reserve |
| How many | For how many |
| take a phone number | have your phone number, have a contact number |
| it's | you can get me on / contact me on |

**3**  Students' own dialogues should be very similar to the one in exercise 1. You could suggest underlining the parts of the dialogue that they need to change (the name of the restaurant, the day and time, the number of people, their name, and the telephone number). Students shouldn't need to write the new dialogue out again in full. They should try to memorize it.

**Teaching tip  Back to back**

Particularly when practising telephone calls, it's a good idea to sit students back to back. This means that, as in real life, they cannot see each other and have to use language alone to communicate. When they have memorized and practised their dialogues in pairs, they can change partners to perform them back to back. That means that the 'waiter' knows more or less what to expect, but not all the details. You can also ask them to write down the booking for an extra challenge. At the end of the call, they can confirm the booking, e.g. *Right, that's a table for six for Lambeth at 8.30 this evening*.

## Can you remember ...?

You can use these sections before or after the **Speak out**, or as revision prompts.

## Speak out

**1**  This is a chance for students to use the language from the lesson in a short piece of writing. They may find there are still one or two extra words or phrases that they need, but try not to introduce too many new words at this stage. Write any generally useful words that come up on the board. This should take no more than ten minutes.

## Alternative

If you think there is a possibility that some students might choose the same restaurant, you can put them in pairs to help each other write. When it comes to exercise 3, they can then change groups.

**2**  Students shouldn't worry about memorizing word for word but, equally, they shouldn't be referring to their text all the time. The idea of writing a text first is to give them a chance to collect their thoughts and make sure they have the vocabulary they need. You could suggest they write down e.g. ten words from their description to help them remember it.

**3**  You may want to convert the prompts into questions on the board before the group work. Encourage the students to add their own questions as they listen to each other. Monitor the group work, and make a note of any errors you want to come back to.

**Feedback:** you can ask individuals to tell you about a restaurant they've just been told about.

**Don't forget**

Practice exercises, Classbook, *p.96*

Teacher's Resource Pack activity 17, *DESIGN A RESTAURANT*

# 18
# SATURDAY & SUNDAY

## Lesson aims

- Revise and practise the past simple irregular and regular.
- Focus on the pronunciation of *-ed* in the past simple.
- Give students the opportunity to talk about last weekend.

## What do you know?

### Note

Students are expected to have met the past simple before. The **What do you know?** section gives them a chance to demonstrate what they know and gives you a chance to assess that knowledge. The past simple tends to be a problem for two reasons:
- It has regular and irregular forms.
- The *-ed* ending is pronounced in three different ways.

Both these areas are looked at in this lesson.

1 With a reasonably strong class, you may want to do this in pairs. Otherwise, do it as a class activity. Point out that the first question is correct. All the other verbs are (incorrectly) in the present simple. Ask what tense they should be in. Then, in pairs, give students time to think about the past forms.

A  How was your weekend?
B  Great! I **had** a fantastic time. On Saturday morning I **played** tennis, then I **went** to the cinema with Angela in the evening.
A  What **did** you see?
B  *Point Blank*. I **thought** it **was** great. We **met** Rachel in the pub afterwards. What about yours?
A  Not bad. Alison **came** around. I **made** dinner for her. She **cooked** for me last week.

2 **Against the clock.** Give students three minutes to brainstorm in pairs and write down more irregular verbs (infinitive and past).

   **Feedback:** go through the answers, and elicit more irregular verbs. Point out that there is a list of common irregular verbs on *p.111* of the Classbook.

| irregular verbs in exercise 1 | |
|---|---|
| be | was |
| have | had |
| go | went |
| do | did |
| think | thought |
| meet | met |
| come | came |
| make | made |

3 Having looked at irregular verbs, ask students to complete the rule about regular verbs.

In the past simple all regular verbs finish in the letters *-ed*.

## Alternative

You may want to revise the verb *to be* now and remind students that it is unique in form. Alternatively, you could leave this until after the listening in **Grammar**, (see the language box in the margin) when they will have come across the different forms.

## Grammar

### Past simple

1 Before concentrating on the grammar, it's a good idea to give the students an opportunity to listen for gist in order to give the dialogue a context. Tell the students that they are going to hear a conversation between two friends (Bruce and Vic). Play the tape / CD and ask what they are talking about (the weekend). Then play the tape / CD again while students read the Tapescript on *p.109* and circle the irregular verbs.

See Tapescript for answers.

| | |
|---|---|
| Bruce | Hi, Vic. How **was** your weekend? |
| Vic | Well, I **came** to the office on Saturday morning, but I **had** a great time after that. |
| Bruce | What **did you do**? |
| Vic | It **was** non-stop – tennis, pub, cinema ... |
| Bruce | What film **did you see**? |
| Vic | *Go*. It **was** brilliant. Sarah **didn't think** so – she **thought** it **was** awful. Anyway ... We **went** to the pub afterwards and **met** Alison. And she **gave** me a birthday present ... for the first time! Why **didn't you come** with us? I **told** you about it. |
| Bruce | I tried to phone you, but you **weren't** in. Karen **came** round for dinner. |
| Vic | How **did it go**? |
| Bruce | A disaster. I **made** fish pie but I **left** it in the oven too long. It **didn't come** out very well ... |
| Vic | Oh. |
| Bruce | Then we **had** a row and Karen **left** early. Not a very good evening ... |

2 Students call out *Stop* when they hear a question or a negative, and write it down.

| negatives | didn't think, weren't, didn't come (out) |
|---|---|
| questions | How was your weekend? What did you do? What film did you see? Why didn't you come with us? How did it go? |

### Teaching tip  Listening for detail

If students are having trouble hearing the complete phrases or questions, write the words they can hear on the board with gaps for the missing words. When you play the tape / CD again, tell them to listen for the missing words.

Draw students' attention to the language box in the margin. They have seen both past forms of the verb *to be* in exercises 1 and 2 but may not have understood that they have the same infinitive. This is a good opportunity to revise the form of *to be*.

**3** Without listening again, students work alone or in pairs.

**Feedback:** ask students to give evidence for their answers.

| | |
|---|---|
| 1 | T |
| 2 | T |
| 3 | F (she thought it was awful) |
| 4 | F (they went to the cinema and the pub) |
| 5 | F (she gave him a present) |
| 6 | F (Bruce phoned Vic) |
| 7 | T |
| 8 | F (Bruce made fish pie) |
| 9 | F (it was a disaster) |

## Grammar box: Past simple

Refer students to the language box, which covers negatives and questions. As a useful mnemonic, negatives follow the pattern Person, Helper, Verb or PHV. The 'helper' is the auxiliary. Questions use Helper, Person, Verb or HPV. In all tenses, the helper determines the tense. Remind students that in negatives and questions the main verb is always in the infinitive.

## Practice

**1** This is a quick activity to test students' knowledge of irregular past forms. Refer to the tip box in the margin for the scoring system of tennis. It's a good idea to demonstrate this with a strong student or ask two students to demonstrate it for the class.

**2** Tell the class that Karen and Sarah are Vic and Bruce's girlfriends (see **Grammar**, exercise 3). The dialogue is their version of the same evening.

In groups of four, Pair A completes Part 1 and Pair B completes Part 2. To check their ideas, suggest they read the dialogues together to see if their verbs fit. You can then put the students into A / B pairs to look at the other part and check each other's work.

**3** Students check their answers with the tape / CD.

**Feedback:** refer students to the Tapescript on *p.109* to confirm their answers. Give them the opportunity to read and listen again if anybody is still having problems.

See Tapescript for answers.

**Part 1**

| | |
|---|---|
| Karen | Hi there, Sarah. |
| Sarah | Oh, hi. How **was** your weekend? How **was** the romantic dinner with Bruce? |
| Karen | It **wasn't** a great success. I **went** round to his place, and he **made** dinner for me, but it **was** horrible. And then we **had** a row. In the end I **left** at about 9.30. |
| Sarah | Oh dear. |
| Karen | Yeah, well. What about you? What **did** you **do**? |

**Part 2**

| | |
|---|---|
| Sarah | I **went** to the pictures with Vic. We **saw** a film called *Go*. I don't recommend it! Vic really **liked** it, but I **thought** it **was** terrible. |
| Karen | **Did** you see Alison? |
| Sarah | Yeah, we **met** her in the pub, and she **gave** Vic a CD for his birthday, so he **was** very pleased! Pity you **weren't** there ... |
| Karen | You can say that again ... |

**4** Students listen to you or the tape / CD and repeat the verbs. If you're using the phonetic alphabet with your class, include it here to clarify the three different pronunciations.

opened
finished
started

| | | |
|---|---|---|
| 1 | opened | /d/ |
| 2 | finished | /t/ |
| 3 | started | /ɪd/ |

**Note**

The *-ed* ending is pronounced as follows:

/d/ after vowels and voiced consonants (tried = /traɪd/, used = /juːzd/)

/t/ after unvoiced consonants (stopped = /stɒpt/)

/ɪd/ after /d/ and /t/ (ended = /'endɪd/, started = /'stɑːtɪd/)

**5** Tell the students to copy the table into their notebooks. In pairs, ask them to decide which column each verb should go in by saying the verbs and listening to each other.

**Feedback:** to check their ideas and drill correct pronunciation, call out the infinitives of the verbs at random to elicit the past simple. Students can also practise in the same way in pairs.

| | | |
|---|---|---|
| 1 | /d/ | showed, lived, travelled |
| 2 | /t/ | stopped, worked |
| 3 | /ɪd/ | decided, wanted, needed |

**Teaching tip** Creating a context

Pronunciation of discrete items is always useful. However, it is essential that students also practise longer utterances. To this end, ask students to write short sentences with some of the verbs in the box and then practise saying the complete sentences. Better still, if time allows (or as homework), students could write short dialogues including some of the verbs and practise them with a partner.

Refer students to the tip box in the margin and ask them to add another example of phrases using *last* and *ago*. Elicit a few sentences using their phrases from the class.

**6** Ask students to make true sentences using *last* or *ago*.

**Feedback:** whole class. Give an example of the last time you did something, and see who has done it more recently. For example:

**Teacher** I went out for dinner a week ago.

**Student A** Well, I went out for dinner three days ago.

**Student B** Well, I went out for dinner last night.

Can you remember ...?

You can use these sections before or after the **Speak out**, or as revision prompts.

## Speak out

1  **Against the clock.** In pairs, give students two minutes each to ask and answer about their weekends. This activity challenges students to think closely about what they did at the weekend and to use a variety of different verbs. Draw students' attention to the tip box in the margin before starting, and suggest they vary their questions. Make sure that they take notes as well as counting the answers. They will need to know what their partner said for exercise 2. If their partner's grammar is wrong, they can say *Sorry?* to indicate a mistake. Be on hand to help.

### Alternative

To get the ball rolling, you can invite students to put you on the spot, firing questions as fast as they can. It also gives them a chance to practise saying the different questions. They can then try to match your score when they do it themselves.

2  As the focus is on past simple question forms, remind the students of the word order (Helper / Auxiliary, Person, Verb), and, if you feel it's necessary, demonstrate by telling the students to ask you more questions about something you did at the weekend. Monitor and collect useful errors for a correction slot.

**Feedback:** find out if anyone did anything interesting or unusual at the weekend. Get students to tell the class about their partner's activities.

### Extra

As a follow up to this lesson you could ask students to write a diary in English. They could do their first entry in the lesson, if you have time, or as homework. Encourage them to bring the diary to class if they want you to check it. You can also use their diaries for a quick warmer; students can briefly look back at their diary entries for the previous day, then ask and answer about their activities. Students can write as much or as little as they want, but encourage them to stretch their vocabulary (using dictionaries) and to write freely, without worrying too much about mistakes.

**Don't forget**

Practice exercises, Classbook, *p.96*

Teacher's Resource Pack activity 18a, *EXCUSES AND EXPLANATIONS*

Teacher's Resource Pack activity 18b, *VERB BUILDING*

## Lesson aims

- Revise and practise vocabulary of regions and countries.
- Practise describing places.
- Focus on comparative adjectives.

## Speak for yourself

**1** Students can work in pairs or groups. The emphasis is on widely-accepted divisions of the world.

**Feedback:** you could use an OHT of the map and ask students to name the areas.

| | |
|---|---|
| 1 | North America |
| 2 | Europe |
| 3 | the Middle East |
| 4 | Asia |
| 5 | the Far East |
| 6 | south-east Asia |
| 7 | Australasia |
| 8 | Africa |
| 9 | South America |
| 10 | Central America |

**2** You could do this as a timed activity. Give students three minutes to think of a country for each region.

**Feedback:** if you already have an OHT of the map on the board, you can list the countries within each region (or ask students to do this). Alternatively, make a list on the board under the appropriate headings, checking spelling and pronunciation as you go along. In a multilingual class, make sure that all the students call out their own countries.

**Possible answers**

| | |
|---|---|
| South America | Brazil, Argentina |
| the Far East | Japan, China |
| the Middle East | Saudi Arabia, Yemen |
| south-east Asia | Thailand, Vietnam |
| Europe | France, Italy |
| Australasia | Australia, New Zealand |
| Africa | Kenya, South Africa |
| Central America | El Salvador, Guatemala |
| Asia | India, Mongolia |
| North America | the United States, Canada |

**3** Make sure that students understand the question. There may be confusion about the difference between *I like going* and *I'd like to go*. Make it clear that they are talking about a country they haven't been to, that it is a dream they have for the future (*One day ...*). You can start by giving your own example.
*One day, I'd like to go to Thailand because it has very beautiful beaches.*

### EXPAND your vocabulary

This can be done as a team game. Divide the class into two or three teams. Explain that you will call out the name of a country. Team members should confer on the language and nationality for that country. When they *all* know the answer, they buzz. You can then ask anyone in the team to answer.

A correct answer gets two points. A wrong answer means another team can answer for one bonus point. Note the ones that students had problems with and make a class list, or ask students to research the answers in a dictionary and make their own lists. Remind students to add new words to their vocabulary books.

## Vocabulary

### Describing places

**1** In pairs, students solve the anagrams to find adjectives that are useful for describing places.

| | |
|---|---|
| clean | hot |
| beautiful | comfortable |
| crowded | noisy |
| polluted | sunny |
| green | expensive |
| touristy | flat |

### Alternative

Ask students to close their books and do one of the following:
- Write the first few letters of each adjective on the board (or dictate them) and ask students to complete the words.
- Write the anagrams (without the first letters) on the board and ask students to solve them.
- Divide the class into A / B pairs. Give all the A students the anagrams and all the B students the first few letters of each word. Individually, students work on the words and then get together with their partner. They can match up their answers and help each other to solve any remaining words. Remind Bs to use the anagrams to check spelling.

**2** Working in the same pairs, students look at the adjectives in exercise 2 and find the opposites from among the adjectives in exercise 1. Ask the students to say the adjectives together and mark the stress.

**Feedback:** you could check students' ideas and pronunciation by asking them to work in open pairs. It's useful to write the words on the board as students call them out so they can check spelling and stress symbols.

| | |
|---|---|
| ugly | beautiful |
| cheap | expensive |
| uncomfortable | comfortable |
| cold | hot |
| quiet | noisy, crowded (touristy) |
| cloudy | sunny |
| mountainous | flat |

**Teaching tip**  Pronunciation

Make sure that students work in pairs when doing a pronunciation exercise, e.g. marking stress on words or in sentences. Emphasize that they must decide on correct pronunciation by saying the words or phrases out loud and listening to each other (not by saying them in their heads, silently). Disagreements can be cleared up by referring to a dictionary or in feedback sessions.

**3** Students can work alone (and then compare with a partner) or in pairs to think of nouns to go with the adjectives in exercise 1.

**Feedback:** put students' words on the board if they need help with spelling or pronunciation.

**Possible answers**

| | |
|---|---|
| clean | streets, beaches |
| beautiful | countryside, cities |
| crowded | streets, beaches, markets |
| polluted | cities, river, sea |
| green | fields, mountains |
| touristy | island, resorts |
| hot | weather, country |
| comfortable | hotel, buses |
| noisy | cities, restaurant |
| sunny | weather, climate, country |
| expensive | restaurant, shops |
| flat | landscape, countryside |

**4** Ask students to look at the pictures and guess which countries they are and why. Remind the students to use vocabulary from the previous exercises.

**Feedback:** you can either tell the students if their guesses are correct or tell them to listen to the tape / CD to confirm their ideas.

**5** Tell students to listen to Lucy talking about her holiday and tick the adjectives she uses. Play the tape / CD again, and ask students to listen for the nouns that are described by each adjective. Are they the ones they chose in exercise 3?

| | |
|---|---|
| beautiful | cities |
| crowded | beaches |
| sunny | weather |
| hot | weather |
| comfortable | hotels |
| (not) expensive | hotels |

| | |
|---|---|
| Jan | You're looking brown. Where've you been? |
| Lucy | I've just got back from Australia and New Zealand. |
| Jan | Wow! You lucky thing! How long were you there for? |
| Lucy | Nearly a month altogether – the first two weeks in Australia, and then a week and a half in New Zealand. |
| Jan | What was it like? |
| Lucy | Absolutely fantastic. Australia was great – beautiful cities, brilliant night life, wonderful beaches, but a bit crowded ... |
| Jan | What was the weather like? |
| Lucy | Sunny every day! It was *so* hot. I got sunburn the first day, and I needed factor 20 for days! |
| Jan | Where did you stay? |
| Lucy | Actually, in some very comfortable hotels, and they weren't expensive either. |

**Note**

The adjectives Lucy uses to express her opinion, e.g. *wonderful*, *brilliant*, *fantastic*, are covered in lesson 10.

# Grammar

## Comparatives

**1** Students listen for the comparative adjectives that Lucy uses to describe New Zealand. These adjectives have already been covered in **Vocabulary**, exercises 1 and 2.

See Tapescript for answers.

| | |
|---|---|
| Jan | How about New Zealand? |
| Lucy | New Zealand was much **quieter** than Australia. The countryside is a lot **greener** and **more mountainous**. Unfortunately it's a lot **cloudier**, too, but we thought it was **more beautiful**. |
| Jan | 'We'? Who's 'we'? |
| Lucy | Secret ... |

## Grammar box: Comparatives

Refer students to the grammar box. Recap the meaning of *syllable*. First, ask students to find the comparatives of the adjectives at the top of the box. Make sure they know which of the adjectives in the flow chart they resemble. You can then copy the chart onto the board and ask students to find other adjectives from the **Vocabulary** section to go in each pattern, 1, 2, or 3+. Alternatively, call out a variety of adjectives and ask students which pattern they follow.

| | | |
|---|---|---|
| 1 | greener | hotter |
| 2 | cloudier | more crowded |
| 3+ | more polluted | |

**Possible answers**

| | | |
|---|---|---|
| 1 | flatter, cleaner | |
| 2 | noisier, sunnier | |
| 3+ | more comfortable, more expensive | |

**Note**

Students may be confused by the use of *like* in the questions in exercise 2. Ask the class where the verb is in the question (*was*) and what the question words are (*what ... like?*). Emphasize that *like* is not a verb in this structure, and point out that it is not used in the answer. You may want to put the following structure on the board: Question: *What ... like?* Answer: *Adjective*.

**2** Students think about Jan's questions, then check in the Tapescript.

**Feedback:** focus on the pronunciation of the questions. Write them on the board and ask students where the strong and weak forms are. Give students the chance to repeat them a few times.

What was it like?
What was the weather like?

Draw students' attention to the language box in the margin, which also shows students how to ask the question in the present tense. (Alternatively, you could elicit the present form of the question.)

## Practice

**1** Students work alone to make questions and match them to the answers.

**Feedback:** let students check in pairs before checking as a class. Write the complete questions on the board for students to refer to in exercise 2.

> **1** What was the flight like?
> It was fine, only two hours.
> **2** What was the hotel like?
> Really comfortable. The bed was enormous.
> **3** What was the food like?
> Very tasty. Lots of fresh fruit, too.
> **4** What were the beaches like?
> Clean, quiet, and beautiful, and the sea was warm.
> **5** What were the people like?
> Very friendly and helpful.

**2** Ask the students to ask and answer the same questions in pairs, but giving negative answers. Indicate the example, and ask students to suggest other negative answers for the same question. Monitor for appropriate responses.

**Feedback:** ask students for some of their ideas. You could ask students to do this in open pairs (see **Teaching tip** on open pairs on *p.57*).

Before doing exercise 3, draw attention to the language box in the margin, or put the three adjectives on the board and find out if the students know what the comparative forms are. Elicit example sentences or questions from the class and practise the pronunciation.

**3** Students work together to order and punctuate the sentences. You could add challenge by doing this as a timed activity, giving students three to five minutes to do the exercise in pairs.

**Feedback:** the focus here is on creating grammatically correct sentences, but draw attention to the weak *than* /ðən/ and encourage students to repeat the sentences after you, copying the rhythm.

> **Possible answers**
> **1** The weather in Britain is worse than in Spain.
> (This is subjective and depends where you live in either country. It also depends what kind of weather you like.)
> **2** The Pacific is larger than the Atlantic.
> **3** Which do you think is more interesting, Tokyo or Seoul / Seoul or Tokyo?
> **4** Shopping in New York is more expensive than in Cape Town.
> **5** It is sunnier in Greece than in Belgium.

### Can you remember …?

You can use these sections before or after the **Speak out**, or as revision prompts.

## Speak out

**1** Ask students to copy the letters onto a piece of paper, or dictate them. These letters reflect the target vocabulary in the lesson.

### Alternative

For an ambitious class, you could suggest pairs make their own list of letters, referring to the vocabulary in the lesson and their own ideas. They can then pass their list to another pair for exercise 2.

**2** Without referring to their books, ask students to write at least one adjective for each letter in their list. You could do this as a challenge to see which pair can finish first.

**Feedback:** students call out each adjective one by one with its comparative.

### Extra

Once the students have finished their lists, they can test each other. Put each pair with another pair. Pair A starts and defines a word on their list for Pair B to guess. They can do this in a number of ways:
- give a synonym
- give the opposite
- give a sentence with the adjective missing
- give a short definition

This should help to reinforce the vocabulary before they use it in exercise 3.

### Alternative

To demonstrate exercise 3, you may want to choose two cities that you are familiar with. This can be very interesting for students, especially if you compare your home town with the one you are teaching in, for example:

Athens is bigger than Edinburgh.

The weather is hotter in Athens than in Edinburgh.

Athens is noisier and more crowded than Edinburgh.

Edinburgh is more expensive than Athens.

**3** Working alone, ask students to think of two cities they know reasonably well. They should think about how these two cities are similar and how they are different.

When they are ready, students get into A / B pairs. Student A compares the two cities, using appropriate adjectives and comparatives. Student B listens and ticks off the adjectives used on the list compiled in exercise 1. Then students change roles.

**Feedback:** ask students to call out the names of some of the cities they talked about. Write them in random order on the board. Ask students to make sentences comparing any of the cities on the board. When a student makes a mistake, throw it open to the class to correct.

> **Don't forget**
> Practice exercises, Classbook, *p.98*
> Teacher's Resource Pack activity 19a, *MY TOWN*
> Teacher's Resource Pack activity 19b, *TWO CITIES*

## Lesson aims

- Study and practise airport and in-flight vocabulary.
- Focus on travel advertisements.
- Practise booking flights.

## Vocabulary challenge

1 You can begin this section with a discussion on holidays. Ask the students where they went for their most recent holiday, and then steer the conversation towards flying and airports. In this way some of the vocabulary from this task should come up, saving time on vocabulary research later.

Once the students get down to the task of reading and discovering any unfamiliar vocabulary, let them confer with each other as well as asking you.

### Extra

Draw a basic picture of an airport on the board (or an OHT) illustrating most of the key vocabulary. Put the students in groups of three to match the words in bold to the things in the picture, or do it as a class. Give students time to copy the picture into their vocabulary books if they want to. You can deal with pronunciation problems as you go along. This is a simple, quick way of dealing with new topic-based vocabulary.

---

**Teaching tip** Testing vocabulary

Once students have had a chance to look up or discuss new vocabulary, they can be tested in a number of ways:

- If you have used a picture and have labelled the picture with the target vocabulary, rub the words out and test the students to see how much they can remember.

- Ask students to close their books, and write the first letter of the highlighted words on the board to see what they can remember, for example:

  p c       passport control
  i-f m     in-flight movie / meals
  b p       boarding pass
  Students can also test each other in the same way.

- Tell students to choose three of the words or phrases each and play hangman in pairs or groups of three.

---

2 Now ask students to order the sentences. Point out the example first, or elicit the first two things. You could add challenge by doing this as a timed activity, giving students three minutes to order the sentences in pairs. If students work in pairs, they are more likely to use the new vocabulary while discussing the order.

Feedback: tell the students to read the text again in the correct order. They can do this alone or as a class so you can check their pronunciation. Then ask them to cover the text or close their books to see what they can remember. To do this, you can go round the class in order, or ask any student who thinks they can remember what comes next. It is not important for the students to remember the sentences word for word. As long as the key vocabulary and the gist of the sentences is there, that is enough. However,

ask students to listen for mistakes and to correct each other where possible.

1 He booked his flight on the Internet.
2 He packed three suitcases.
3 He went to the airport by taxi.
4 He checked in and got his boarding pass.
5 He went through passport control.
6 He waited for three hours in the departure lounge.
7 He went to the gate and got on the plane.
8 The plane took off.
9 He watched the in-flight movie and ate two in-flight meals.
10 The plane landed and he got off.
11 He went through passport control again.
12 He picked up his luggage and walked into the arrival hall.

### Alternative

Put the students into three groups and play this as a game. Go from group to group and ask them for the next stage in the sequence. (You can vary the number of groups, but make sure that each group has an equal number of stages.) Give two points for correct answers and allow bonuses.

3 Students work in pairs to recycle language from exercise 1.

### EXPAND your vocabulary

Draw students' attention to the **Expand your vocabulary** box. Ask them to cover exercise 1 and complete the exercise in pairs, or do it on the board. You could expand this by telling students to choose two more sentences from exercise 1, copy them with gaps for the verbs, and test a partner. To avoid students choosing the same sentences, tell As to choose sentences from 1 to 6 and Bs to choose from 7 to 12. Remind students to record their new words in this way in their vocabulary books.

---

I **booked** my flight.
I **packed** my suitcase.
I **went through** passport control.
I **got on** / **off** the plane.
I **watched** the in-flight movie.
The plane **landed**.

---

## English in use
### Booking by phone

1 Give students a time limit of two minutes to glance over the advert, as initially they only need to understand the gist of the text.

Feedback: in groups or as a class. Ask students if their preference would be Barcelona or Reykjavik, and why. The 'why' part is the most important, as it will allow you to see what information they have gleaned from the text. If they add their own knowledge of either place, that is fine.

**Teaching tip** Predicting

Begin the task with a general discussion about Barcelona and Reykjavik. Have any of the students visited either city? What do they know about the two places? You could even ask what students think they would find in an advert for holidays in both cities. Eliciting information in this way, before students look at the text, will prepare them for the reading, provide an in-built reading task (comparing their ideas with the text), and give them more to say when justifying their choice of which city to visit.

**Note**

Unfamiliar vocabulary in the text is likely to be: midnight, take advantage of, last-minute deals, seductive, as well as, sights, easy access, spectacular, northernmost, hippest, discount, car rental, available, fares, subject to availability, inclusive, conditions apply

2   Students now read the advert in greater detail. Allow students to use dictionaries, and go round helping with any difficult vocabulary.

   **Feedback:** when students give their answers, make sure they justify them with reference to the text, as in the key.

   1   F (*£3 discount* for booking online)
   2   F (Tickets are *from £65 rtn*)
   3   F (The city is *full of life*)
   4   T (There is *24-hour sunshine in the summer*)
   5   T (It has *the hippest nightclubs in Europe*)
   6   T (*Fantastic deals on car rental*)
   7   F (You can phone on *0845 6871111*)

**Teaching tip** Dictionary work

To vary dictionary work, try the following:

   •   Finding the meaning of words becomes a race. The first student / pair / group to finish is tested by the rest of the class to see if they really do know the meanings.

   •   Share out the words to be looked up among the class or groups. Everybody is responsible for finding out the meaning of their word and how to use it. They must then teach the word to the class or a new group.

   •   Put students into groups and allow them to use dictionaries to look up any words they wish from a text. Once they have finished, groups can challenge each other to define and explain any words from the text.

3   Ask the students to work alone for this exercise.
   **Feedback:** in pairs before checking answers as a class.

   1   I'd like **to book** a flight, please.
   2   15 July, if **possible**.
   3   Just **myself / me**.
   4   Sometime **in the morning**.
   5   By **credit card**, please.
   6   **06** / 05.
   7   Yes, it's **11 Greendykes Road, Charlbury, OX7 3QQ**

   Ask students (in pairs) to discuss how to say the dates in the table before doing exercise 4. Then look at the tip box in the margin dealing with the 24-hour clock.

4   Before listening, get students to read through the table. Then ask them questions using the prompts, giving students the opportunity to feedback the information in the table. This will prime students for the **Speak out**, as well as helping when listening for mistakes, as it allows you to focus on pronunciation of important items, e.g. the difference between *fifteen* and *fifty*.

   **Feedback:** in pairs before checking answers as a class.

| where? | Barcelona |
| --- | --- |
| date / leave? | 15 June |
| date / come back? | 1 July |
| time / leave? | 8.20 |
| time / come back? | 15.15 |
| price | £90 |

**Part 1**

| | |
| --- | --- |
| Travel agent | Hello, Timetravel, Andy speaking, how can I help you? |
| Ms McCall | Oh hello, I'd like to book a flight, please. |
| Travel agent | Where to? |
| Ms McCall | To Barcelona. |
| Travel agent | And when would you like to travel? |
| Ms McCall | 15 June, if possible. |
| Travel agent | And coming back? |
| Ms McCall | The first of July. |
| Travel agent | And how many people is that for? |
| Ms McCall | Just me. |
| Travel agent | OK, bear with me for a moment ... We've got flights on the fifteenth at 08.20 arriving 10.50 and at 16.40 arriving 19.20. |
| Ms McCall | The 08.20 would be good. |
| Travel agent | And coming back on the first there's 09.00 arriving 11.15 or 15.15 arriving 17.50. |
| Ms McCall | The 15.15, please. |
| Travel agent | OK. |
| Ms McCall | And could you tell me how much that is, please? |
| Travel agent | Yes, sure. It'll be £90, which includes airport tax. |
| Ms McCall | OK, that's fine. |
| Travel agent | How would you like to pay? |

5   Ask students to listen to the second part and complete the booking form as if they were travel agents. You will probably need to play the tape / CD twice.

**Part 2**

| | |
| --- | --- |
| Travel agent | How would you like to pay? |
| Ms McCall | Visa, please. |
| Travel agent | Could I have the number? |
| Ms McCall | It's 4929 4781 3111. |
| Travel agent | And the expiry date? |
| Ms McCall | 07/06. |
| Travel agent | And the holder's name? |
| Ms McCall | RS McCall, that's M, small c, capital C, A, double L. |
| Travel agent | Great. So that's a return to Barcelona, leaving 15 June 08.20, returning 1 July 15.15. |
| Ms McCall | Yeah, that's right. |
| Travel agent | OK. If I could give you a reference number. It's CT 12435. Please quote that number if you have any queries. Could you confirm your address and postcode? |
| Ms McCall | Yes, it's 22 Castle Road, Edinburgh. |
| Travel agent | And the postcode? |
| Ms McCall | EH8 7DS. |
| Travel agent | Fine. The ticket will be in the post – you should get it tomorrow. |
| Ms McCall | Thanks, bye. |
| Travel agent | Bye. |

6   Ask students to compare their answers in pairs.

| Card holder | RS McCall |
| --- | --- |
| Visa number | 4929 4781 3111 |
| Expiry date | 07 / 06 |
| Booking reference | CT12435 |
| Address | 22 Castle Road, Edinburgh |
| Postcode | EH8 7DS |

**Teaching tip** Listening

Vary the way you present listening texts. Rather than play the whole text, tell students to stop you as soon as they hear the answer. You can select students to do this, or tell students to call out when they hear the answer. Students tell you the answer, then you continue to the next question. At the end replay the whole text as confirmation.

## Can you remember ...?

You can use these sections before or after the **Speak out**, or as revision prompts.

## Speak out

1  Ask everybody to read through the role play, dealing with any problems. Then divide the class into customers (As) and travel agents (Bs).

2  Allow students to prepare their roles alone, in pairs, or in groups. Give them a time limit, as the activity should be relatively spontaneous. Remind them to go back through the lesson noting any useful vocabulary.

3  Put the students into A / B pairs, sitting back to back. Let them practise together at first, then ask willing pairs to come and perform their phone call from memory in front of the class.

**Feedback:** be positive about students' performances. The occasion could also be used for error correction. As the students perform their dialogues, collect any mistakes and go through them at the end.

**Teaching tip** Performing dialogues

Before students begin practising, tell them that you will ask some of them to perform their dialogues after they have finished. This should motivate them while they are practising. It also gives students who are unwilling to perform the chance to let you know before you ask them in front of the class.

**Don't forget**

Practice exercises, Classbook, *p.99*

Teacher's Resource Pack activity 20, *AIRPORTS*

## Lesson aims

- Introduce and practise vocabulary for describing accommodation.
- Focus on signs and abbreviations for accommodation.
- Practise booking a hotel room.

## Speak for yourself

### Note

Unfamiliar vocabulary in the exercise is likely to be: self-catering, camper van, guest-houses

1  Before students open their books, begin the activity by asking them where they like staying when they are on holiday. This will indicate what vocabulary they already know. If possible, get them to explain why they choose that kind of accommodation. This will prime them for the written exercise to follow.

Then draw attention to the types of accommodation listed in the activity and the pictures. This is a chance to concentrate on any vocabulary they have not already come up with.

### Extra

Following the activity, you can test students' knowledge of the vocabulary by asking them a number of questions, for example:
*What is the most expensive / cheapest form of accommodation?*
*What can you use if you don't want to stay in one place?*
*What can you book if you want to cook for yourself?*
*What is like a hotel but cheaper?*
This can be done with books open or closed.

2  Students now write about how they feel about the different types of accommodation. They can write as many sentences as they like, or you can specify the number. Focus on the examples before they begin. As they write, move around the classroom supplying any vocabulary and helping with any difficulties. Don't worry if some of the sentences are not perfect. As long as the message is clear, that is enough for the following activity.

### Teaching tip  Student accuracy

Sometimes content is more important than accuracy. The main aim of the sentences in exercise 2 is to promote a discussion in exercise 3.

3  Students now get together to share their ideas and take a poll. The size of the groups depends on how you want to divide up your class, but four is recommended.

**Feedback:** ask a spokesperson from each group to tell the class where most people stay when on holiday. You will then get a class favourite.

## Vocabulary

### Understanding accommodation guides

### Note

Unfamiliar vocabulary in the exercise is likely to be: accepted, packed lunches, facilities, en suite, central heating, pets

1  You could do this as a timed activity, with students working alone or in pairs. Give them two minutes to match the symbols for facilities with their descriptions. Try not to help students with the vocabulary. Tell them to use the symbols to guess the meanings. Students could say what they think the symbols mean before they match them with the descriptions.

| | |
|---|---|
| 1 | no smoking |
| 2 | central heating |
| 3 | credit cards accepted |
| 4 | rooms with television |
| 5 | packed lunches |
| 6 | number of en suite rooms |
| 7 | tea / coffee facilities |
| 8 | pets welcome |

2  Students can now test each other on the meaning of the symbols. Encourage them to ask and answer using complete sentences, and show them the example. If they are already in pairs, it would be better to get them to change partners here.

3  Give students a couple of minutes to read through the advertisements. Allow them to help each other with difficult vocabulary, use dictionaries, or ask you. When they are familiar with the texts, ask them to write a sentence outlining which guest-house they prefer and why. Encourage them to include a number of reasons.

Before they begin, point out the skeleton sentence in the book. As they write, move around the classroom helping where necessary. Once again, content is more important than accuracy. So long as students can express themselves clearly, that is enough to be able to complete the next activity.

4  Students now get into groups to discuss their ideas.
**Feedback:** once students have had a chance to discuss their ideas, you could conduct a class poll to see which is the more popular guest-house. You can also tell them which accommodation you would choose and why.

### Teaching tip  Class polls

You can conduct class polls in a number of ways:
- Ask students to put their hands up for you to count.
- Ask students to write their choice on a piece of paper (secret ballot).
- Tell students to stand or sit in a certain part of the classroom as a way of expressing what they think.
- Ask students to come up to the board and indicate their choice by ticking a box or word.

# English in use
## Booking by phone

1 Begin by asking if anybody has been to New York. Where did they stay and what was the accommodation like? Now play the tape / CD and ask them to tell you what it is about, before looking at the sentences in their book. You may need to play the tape / CD twice.

**Feedback:** students can compare their answers in pairs before listening for the second time. Then check as a class.

> 1 They want a room for **this Friday** and **Saturday**.
> 2 They want a **double** room with **en suite bathroom**.
> 3 The room costs **$225**.
> 4 The price includes **breakfast**.

| | |
|---|---|
| Receptionist | Hello, Hotel Excelsior. |
| David | Yes, hello. I'd like to book a room for this Friday and Saturday, please. |
| Receptionist | Certainly, sir, what kind of room would you like? |
| David | A double room with en suite bathroom, please. |
| Receptionist | Yes, we have a double free at $225 with breakfast. |
| David | OK. Can I phone back later to confirm? |
| Receptionist | Yes, that's fine. |
| David | OK, thank you. Goodbye. |
| Receptionist | Goodbye. |

---

**Teaching tip** Listening

To vary the interaction when listening, you can divide up the questions among the students – one group can answer the first question, another group the second question, and so on. When they have finished, rearrange the groups so they can share information (see **Teaching tip** on regrouping students on *p.26*). Normally students will be able to check each other's work, as they will have picked up more than just the answer to their question.

---

2 Students could work alone for this exercise, to allow you to see how much language they have picked up.

> 1 I'd like to book a room for this Friday and Saturday. (David)
> 2 We have a double free at $225 with breakfast. (receptionist)
> 3 Can I phone back later to confirm? (David)

Draw students' attention to the tip box in the margin, or elicit the different types of room from the class.

3 Apart from making a note of the three differences between the two hotels, ask students to make a note of the name of the new hotel (the Majestic). This will help them with the next activity.

**Feedback:** in pairs before checking answers as a class.

> 1 There are no en suite doubles available, only singles.
> 2 The cost of the two singles is $180, a lower price.
> 3 Breakfast is not included.

| | |
|---|---|
| Receptionist | Hello, the Majestic. |
| David | Yes, hello. I'd like to book a double room with en suite bathroom for Friday and Saturday, please. |
| Receptionist | I'm afraid all the en suite doubles are taken, sir. We can offer you two en suite singles. |
| David | How much are the two singles? |
| Receptionist | They're $90 each. |
| David | Is that with breakfast? |

| | |
|---|---|
| Receptionist | No, that's just the rooms. |
| David | OK, thank you. I'll think about it. Goodbye. |
| Receptionist | Goodbye. |

4 Ask the students to listen to a very short conversation to discover which hotel David chooses. It is simply a matter of picking out the name of the hotel. Once they have got the answer, it's a good idea to replay the three conversations with the students following the Tapescripts on *p.109*. This will reinforce the language (see **Teaching tip** on using Tapescripts on *p.29*).

| | |
|---|---|
| Receptionist | Hello, Hotel Excelsior. |
| David | Yes, hello. I'd like to confirm a booking for this Friday and Saturday, please … |

5 Students read the sentences in the **Useful language** box and listen for the stressed words in each sentence. Before they listen, they could practise reading the sentences in pairs, marking the words they think are stressed. They can then listen to check their ideas.

See Tapescript for answers.

> 1 Do you have any rooms free for tomorrow night?
> 2 I'd like to book a double room for Friday and Saturday.
> 3 Can I phone back later to confirm?
> 4 How much is a single?
> 5 Is that with breakfast?
> 6 I'd like to confirm a booking, please.

**Feedback:** whole class.

### Can you remember …?

You can use these sections before or after the **Speak out**, or as revision prompts.

## Speak out

1 You could begin this activity by asking students if anybody has been to South Africa or knows anything about the country. Then put the students into pairs, and ask them to look at their respective pages. Give them about five minutes to prepare their roles.

2 Ask students to sit back to back to conduct their phone calls. When they have finished, the A students should decide which room they want. Give them a time limit of two minutes to make their decision.

3 They should then phone back to confirm their reservation. It is possible some hoteliers won't get any confirmation calls at all. If so, ask these hoteliers to think about or discuss why they think nobody booked their rooms. At the end of the activity, ask A students to give reasons for their choices, and find out if the reasons are the same.

---

**Don't forget**

Practice exercises, Classbook, *p.100*

Teacher's Resource Pack activity 21a, *THE IDEAL HOTEL*

Teacher's Resource Pack activity 21b, *HOLIDAY PROBLEMS*

---

## Lesson aims

- Introduce and practise money vocabulary.
- Study and practise the present perfect and past participles.
- Contrast the present perfect and past simple.
- Give students the opportunity to talk about their experiences.

## What do you know?

1 **Against the clock.** Give students one minute to add words to the chart alone, before working in pairs or groups to create a joint list. Tell them to copy the chart into their books before doing the activity.

| Possible answers | | | |
|---|---|---|---|
| **verbs** | **nouns** | **adjectives** | **people** |
| to pay | cheque | expensive | banker |
| to sell | cash | poor | accountant |
| to lend | coins | cheap | shopper |
| to win | shopping | | |

2 Copy the chart onto the board, and either ask students to call out their words or ask representatives from each group to write up their own words.

**Feedback:** check spelling and pronunciation as you go along.

3 Here, students have the opportunity to test each other by writing gap-fill sentences. The groups should write their sentences on a piece of paper, which will be passed round in exercise 4. You might want groups to write more than one sentence, depending on the time available. Monitor what they are writing, and be available to help.

4 Give each group numbers for their questions and ask students to write all the numbers in the margin of a piece of paper. Get groups to pass their sentences round the class, and ask students to note down their answers against the correct number. Students can work in pairs and then groups to compare.

**Feedback:** any disagreements should be directed to the authors of the sentences. Only help where necessary.

## Grammar

### Present perfect and past simple

You can focus on the box in the margin before or after the exercise, using it to see what the students know, eliciting the ways to carry money suggested in exercise 1, or as a follow-up speaking practice.

1 Make sure that everyone understands the different ways to carry money suggested in the exercise. Students listen and compare in pairs or as a class. Ask students to justify their answers if possible.

Take credit cards and cash. (*I've always taken credit cards … And maybe some cash …*)

**◉1**

| | |
|---|---|
| Alex | Mark, have you ever been to Canada? |
| Mark | Yeah, a few times. I went on a work trip to Toronto last year. Why? |
| Alex | Well, I need your advice. I'm spending three weeks on holiday there next month, and I'm not sure about the best way to take money. |
| Mark | I've always taken credit cards – you can use them everywhere, and you don't need to carry cash around. |
| Alex | Have you ever lost them? |
| Mark | Only once. I left my wallet on a table in a restaurant, and luckily the manager phoned my hotel. |
| Alex | And what about traveller's cheques? |
| Mark | I haven't used them for years. They're OK, and most hotels will change them, but you pay commission when you buy them, it's about 3% … |
| Alex | True. Yeah, it sounds as if credit cards would be best. |
| Mark | Definitely. And maybe some cash, a few hundred dollars, for taxis and things … |
| Alex | OK, well, thanks for the advice. |
| Mark | That's OK – have a good trip! |

2 On the second listening, students focus on the use of the present perfect. You might want to model the phrases first so that the students know what to listen for.

| | |
|---|---|
| Have you ever? | ✓ ✓ |
| I've | ✓ |
| I haven't | ✓ |

3 Ask students to compare what they heard in pairs.

4 Ask students to look at the Tapescript, writing down the words which complete the phrases, making present perfect questions, statements, and negatives.

**Feedback:** when they are ready it's a good idea to play the tape / CD again and let students follow the Tapescript, focusing on pronunciation, especially the contractions.

Have you ever **been to Canada**?
Have you ever **lost them**?
I've **always taken credit cards**.
I haven't **used them for years**.

### Alternative

With a strong class, do this as an intensive listening exercise. Students listen and try to complete each phrase. If they are having difficulties, you can use the board to write up the words as they hear them (see **Teaching tip** on listening for detail on *p.53*).

5 This question is designed to get students thinking about the use of the present perfect compared with the past simple. Refer students to the grammar box for use.

I **left** my wallet on a table in a restaurant. (past simple)

### Grammar box: Present perfect

#### Form

Get students to work with the form of the present perfect first by using the flow chart. It is helpful if you copy the chart onto the board or use an OHT. Call out a verb with a personal pronoun, e.g. *play*, *we*, and ask students to make a sentence using the present perfect, e.g. *We've often played baseball*. Start with regular verbs. You can then ask the students to give you some irregular verbs. Write them on the board in a list with a personal pronoun each, e.g. *go, I* and *eat, you*, e.g. *I've been to America*. Divide the class into pairs and see which pair can make correct sentences first (irregular past participles are on *p.111*). To make it more challenging, you can also add S, N, or Q (statement, negative, or question) after each verb.

**Use**

Look at the conversation in the listening and point out that the present perfect can be used to start a conversation and that the past simple goes on to give more information. You can ask general questions around the class and encourage them to ask you in return, e.g. *Have you ever been to Britain (before)? Have you ever walked 10 miles / kilometres? Have you ever cooked a meal for more than six people?*

## Practice

You can refer students to the tip box in the margin before or after exercise 1. You can ask the students what *once* means in the conversation in exercise 1, and try to elicit the other words and expressions from the class.

1 Students can work alone and check in pairs.

   **Feedback:** write the form of the sentences in order on the board as a reference.

| | |
|---|---|
| A | present perfect question |
| B | brief response |
| A | past simple question |
| B | past simple response |

2 Ask students to complete the chart in pairs – some of the verbs will have come up in the **Speak for yourself** section. Encourage them to use dictionaries to find

out the meanings and, if necessary, to look up the forms of the verbs, too. You could do this as a timed activity, giving students three minutes to complete the chart.

| win | **won** | won |
|---|---|---|
| borrow | borrowed | **borrowed** |
| lend | **lent** | lent |
| **find** | found | found |
| lose | **lost** | lost |
| **give** | gave | **given** |
| buy | **bought** | **bought** |

3 Students practise the tense order that they will need to have a conversation about their experiences. They should do this as quickly as possible.

4 Students now have a chance to practise using the present perfect and past simple in short dialogues, using the questionnaire and the model dialogue below it. This model dialogue fits the pattern that you wrote on the board in exercise 1. Monitor carefully for correct short responses, and for past simple question forms and answers.

   **Feedback:** you could ask strong students to repeat some of the dialogues in open pairs. This will help those who are having problems. You could then go through any common problems on the board.

## Speak out

**Teaching tip**  Making pairs

If the students have been mingling for the previous exercise, you can pair students in one of two ways for exercise 1. Either tell students to stay with the person they last had a conversation with, or ask them to choose someone they think they know quite well. Only use the latter method if you feel that no one will get left out.

1  Ask students to write ten questions for each other, five which they think will get *no* answers, and five which they think will get *yes* answers. They should mix up the *yes* and *no* questions. It may be a good idea to demonstrate this activity, by writing *yes* and *no* on the board. Ask one student to look away while you point to the *yes* on the board for the benefit of the rest of the class, then ask a question. If the student says *no*, evince surprise and disappointment. Do the same with the *no*, using a different student.

2  Students ask and answer to confirm their ideas about each other. Tell students to continue the conversation as long as they can if they get a *yes* answer.

3  Ask students what they learned about each other that surprised them. Were they right in all their ideas about each other?

**Don't forget**

Practice exercises, Classbook, *p.101*

Teacher's Resource Pack activity 22a, *WHAT DO YOU SPEND YOUR MONEY ON?*

Teacher's Resource Pack activity 22b, *THE PERFECT GAME*

# 23
## SHOPS & SHOPPING

### Lesson aims

- Revise and extend shop vocabulary.
- Practise what to say in shops.
- Practise talking about what things are for.

## Speak for yourself

### Alternative

You can introduce different types of shops by doing the **Vocabulary** section before the **Speak for yourself**.

1 Ask students to look at the pictures of shops, and elicit the countries they might be in and why. You can give them a few minutes to think about the questions before they start. As practice, they can ask you the questions about your personal favourite. Students then work together to tell each other about their own favourite shop. Be on hand to help with the names of certain types of shop.

2 After discussing the question in pairs, you can do a class survey to see what type of shop is the most popular. This gives students a chance to check the names of different types of shop.

## Vocabulary

### Shops

1 Ask students to solve the acrostic by listening to the short dialogues. Stop the tape / CD after each two-line dialogue and let students confer in pairs. Play the dialogues again if necessary. If they understand where each dialogue is but don't know the word in English, they can write it beside the acrostic in their language and then check with a partner or use a bilingual dictionary.

**Feedback:** ask students which words gave them the answers.

| | | | |
|---|---|---|---|
| 1 | chemist's | 5 | supermarket |
| 2 | clothes shop | 6 | post office |
| 3 | shoe shop | 7 | bank |
| 4 | bookshop | 8 | newsagent |

See Tapescript for 'clues' in **bold**.

🔊 1

1 A I'd like some **travel sickness pills**, please.
   B We've got them in boxes of 12 or 24.
2 A Have you got this **jacket** in **extra large**?
   B Hold on, I'll just check for you.
3 A Could I try these **boots** on, please?
   B What size are you?
   A I think I'm a **39**.
4 A Have you got any English–**Spanish** dictionaries?
   B Yes, on the **third** floor.
5 A Could you tell me where the **bread** is?
   B Yes, it's in aisle **seven**.

6 A I'd like to send this **letter**, please.
   B First or second class?
7 A How would you like it?
   B Two **tens** and a **twenty**, please.
8 A Have you got any **French** newspapers?
   B No, sorry, we're sold out.

2 Ask students to look at the Tapescript, change the words in bold, and practise the dialogues in pairs. It's a good idea to listen to the tape / CD again for intonation and to practise one or two of the dialogues in chorus first. Monitor carefully for appropriacy.

**Feedback:** ask a few students to make new dialogues in open pairs for the class.

### Extra

Before doing exercise 2, start a rapid word association game by calling out *chemist's – medicine*, and go round the class with students calling out items that are sold there, e.g. *chemist's – medicine, shampoo, soap, aspirin, make-up*, etc. If someone gets stuck, they can call out a new shop, e.g. *bookshop – travel guide*, and the game continues until they've run out of ideas. This should help students with ideas for exercise 2.

## English in use

### What's it for?

1 **Against the clock.** In pairs, give students five minutes to make sentences and match them to the pictures. Make sure that there is one sentence per picture.

| | |
|---|---|
| a | It's for storing information. |
| b | It's for taking pictures. |
| c | They're for sending postcards. |
| d | It's for paying for the shopping. |
| e | It's for looking up new words. |
| f | They're for cutting paper. |
| g | It's for remembering appointments. |
| h | They're for listening to music. |
| i | It's for making calls. |
| j | It's for taking messages. |
| k | They're for locking the door. |
| l | It's for making coffee. |

2 Students compete in pairs to see how many of the objects they know the names of.

**Feedback:** students dictate the answers for you to write on the board. Check that everyone agrees on the spelling. For the unfamiliar words, spell them out letter by letter to see who can guess the word first.

Focus students' attention on the tip box in the margin. Elicit similar plural words, e.g. *headphones, shorts, trousers, tights*.

3 To reinforce the vocabulary of this section, students test each other in pairs. Remind students to use singular and plural correctly.

## EXPAND your vocabulary

You may want to demonstrate this in class by asking students to label everything in the classroom. If you have posters, e.g. of landscapes, in the classroom, students can also label what's in them.

Encourage students to label things at home. You could follow this up by asking students over the next few days what new words around the house they have learned using labels.

## Extra

After labelling the classroom you can do a warmer on the following day. Move all the labels around and ask students to put them in the right place again.

**4** Ask students, in pairs, to write out the phrases in the correct order. Students listen and check.

See Tapescript for answers.

1 Can I help you?
2 Do you mean a camera?
3 What's it called?
4 What are you looking for?
5 I don't know the word in English.
6 I wonder if you could help me, please.
7 Yes, that's it.
8 I don't know what it's called in English.

**5** Ask students to complete the shop dialogues with the phrases from exercise 4. Ask students which statements are interchangeable (5 and 8), and tell them to use a different one in each dialogue.

**6** Students check their answers with the tape / CD. They can then look at the Tapescript and practise the dialogues in pairs. Monitor students' pronunciation as they work together.

See Tapescript for answers.

1
Assistant   Can I help you?
Customer   Yes, I'm looking for something, but I don't know the word in English. It's for putting photographs in.
Assistant   Oh, a photo frame.
Customer   Yes, that's it.

2
Customer   Hello. I wonder if you could help me, please.
Assistant   Of course. What are you looking for?
Customer   That's the problem – I don't know what it's called in English. It's for taking photographs.
Assistant   Do you mean a camera?
Customer   No, the thing in the camera. What's it called?
Assistant   Oh, the film.
Customer   Yes, that's it.

## Can you remember ...?

You can use these sections before or after the **Speak out**, or as revision prompts.

## Speak out

This gives students the opportunity to make up their own dialogues. Rather than writing them down, tell them to practise the dialogues in pairs until they can remember them. Help with pronunciation. Pairs then get into groups of four and act out their dialogues to each other.

**Feedback:** you could ask some students to perform their dialogues for the class.

---

**Teaching tip**  Rehearsing with a tape recorder

When students are practising dialogues, it can be very helpful for them rehearse into a tape recorder. This means they can listen to themselves and self-correct before doing it 'live'. It also means that you don't have to be listening all the time, as they can work independently and then ask you for help when they need it. Obviously, this depends on class size and facilities, but you can get groups of four to share tape recorders. Alternatively, there are a number of activities in the book that lend themselves to students recording themselves, so you can let different students do it each time until everyone has had a turn.

---

**Don't forget**

Practice exercises, Classbook, *p.102*

Teacher's Resource Pack activity 23, *SHOPPING SPREE*

- Revise and extend clothes vocabulary and categories.
- Practise useful language for clothes shopping.
- Give students the opportunity to talk about clothes.

## Vocabulary challenge

1 **Against the clock.** Give students, in pairs, two minutes for A to write down clothes and B to write down colours. If the A students are struggling, encourage them to do quick sketches of the clothes and then use their partner or you to help with the vocabulary.

2 Put pairs into groups of four to help each other to correct and improve their lists. Monitor this stage.

**Feedback:** you can put a class list on the board and get students to practise connecting colours with clothes, e.g. a black sweater, blue jeans, white socks. This will give you an opportunity to check pronunciation.

### Alternative

Put students in AA, BB pairs first to help with spelling and vocabulary before getting into A / B pairs.

### Alternative

A different way to elicit relevant, current clothes vocabulary is to use what the students are wearing. Brainstorm students' clothes (including colours) onto the board, or let students make a list in pairs, and then a class list. If you wish, you can put the clothes into two columns, one for singular and one for plural clothes. After a few examples, ask students the reason for the two columns. They can then tell you which column to put each item of clothing into. The class can then add more ideas to the lists.

3 Using their lists, students tell each other what clothes they took with them on their most recent weekend away. Monitor for pronunciation, word order, and correct use of singular and plural items of clothing.

### Alternatives

1 Ask students to imagine it's a different season, e.g. if it's summer now, imagine it's winter. What clothes would they pack for a weekend away?

2 Elicit different types of trips people can go on, e.g. business trips, a honeymoon, a trekking holiday, a beach holiday. Allot different trips to different pairs, and ask them to talk about the clothes they would take. Students then swap partners and exchange ideas on different clothes for different trips.

## Vocabulary

### What to wear

1 Ask students to match the vocabulary to the pictures.

**Feedback:** check by asking students to describe the pictures. This will give you the opportunity to deal with any pronunciation problems.

1 cargo pants, a jumper, trainers, a cap, a bag
2 a suit, a briefcase
3 a fleece, a waterproof jacket, walking boots, a backpack, gloves

### Extra

The vocabulary in this section is intended to be practical and as up to date as possible. However, as fashions change quite rapidly, you may want to bring in current magazines and ask students to cut out pictures of clothes they are interested in. They can then label the clothes (including colours if they want) and make a class poster of the current fashions.

Focus students on the box in the margin. Find out if students know what a suit is, and elicit two other clothes with suit from the class. These can then be included in exercise 3. You could give students other ways of talking about swimwear if they ask, e.g. swimming costume, bikini, one-piece (all female), and swimming trunks (male).

tracksuit, swimsuit

**Teaching tip** Expanding vocabulary

Encourage students to expand the vocabulary from activities in class, and accept new vocabulary items which students suggest, as long as they are relevant to the activity. You can use one side of the board to make a list of new vocabulary which comes up in class, in addition to the target vocabulary in their books. Students may only learn a small proportion of the vocabulary which comes up in class, but it is important to expose them to as much as possible, and to encourage a proactive attitude in class.

2 Do this as a mingling activity, with students talking to different people about what clothes they have. This gives them the opportunity to practise pronunciation and to use the question form *Have you got ...?* You may want to get students to ask you a few questions first to get the ball rolling.

Draw students' attention to the tip box in the margin. Brainstorm more plural clothes (or remind students of the tip box on *p.71*) and get students to practise using *pair*, e.g. *a pair of shorts, a pair of tights*.

3 Students can work in pairs to put the different clothes in exercise 1 into the Internet shopping site categories. Some clothes may fit into more than one category.

**Feedback:** whole class.

| tops | a jumper, a fleece |
| --- | --- |
| bottoms | cargo pants |
| outerwear | a waterproof jacket, a fleece, gloves |
| footwear | trainers, walking boots |
| swimwear | a swimsuit |
| accessories | a briefcase, a backpack, a bag, gloves, a cap |
| activity | trainers, a tracksuit, a swimsuit, walking boots, a backpack |
| business | a briefcase, a suit |

**4** Students listen and identify the clothes being talked about, then compare their ideas with a partner.

**Feedback:** ask students to identify the word(s) that helped them find the right answer.

1 trainers (*sporty, comfortable*)
2 bag (*everything in it – keys, cheque book*)
3 gloves (*cold hands*)
4 cargo pants (*prefer them to a skirt, all those pockets*)
5 fleece (*light, warm, isn't waterproof*)

1 I'm not very sporty, but everyone wears them – they're just really comfortable.
2 I keep everything in it – keys, cheque book, driving licence, make-up, address book ... I'd be lost without it!
3 I hate having cold hands, so I really love them.
4 I prefer them to a skirt – much more practical, especially with all those pockets.
5 It's very light and very warm, but it lets the wind through and it isn't waterproof.

# English in use
## Going clothes shopping

**1** Ask students to work in pairs to match the phrases to the person who says them in a shop.

1 friend (possibly shop assistant)
2 shop assistant (possibly friend)
3 customer
4 shop assistant
5 customer
6 friend (possibly shop assistant, but unlikely)
7 shop assistant
8 customer
9 customer

**2** Ask students to use the language in exercise 1 to complete the dialogues. They can work in pairs or alone at first, and then check in pairs.

**3** Students listen and confirm their answers. Stop the tape / CD after each exchange. Point out that *Are you all right there?* and *Can I help you?* are interchangeable.

See Tapescript for answers.

**1**
| | |
|---|---|
| **Shop assistant** | Are you all right there? |
| **Customer** | Just looking, thanks. |

**2**
| | |
|---|---|
| **Shop assistant** | Can I help you? |
| **Customer** | Yes, have you got these in a large? |

**3**
| | |
|---|---|
| **Customer** | What do you think? |
| **Friend** | It looks great. |

**4**
| | |
|---|---|
| **Shop assistant** | Any good? |
| **Customer** | Yeah, I'll take this one, please. |

**4** Students listen and practise the dialogues in pairs. You may want to start the activity as a drill, getting the students to repeat the dialogues line by line after the tape / CD.

**5** Students match all the sentences that mean the same thing. This will give them more variety in their dialogues.

| | |
|---|---|
| Can I help you? | Do you need any help? |
| | Are you all right? |
| What do you think? | Any good? |
| | How does it look? |
| It looks great. | It looks really nice. |
| I'll take this one, please. | This one will be fine. |
| | I'd like this one, please. |

**6** Ask the students to change partners and to close their books. They can then practise the dialogues again, using as many of the different phrases as possible.

## Alternative

You could get students to do this in groups of three. Two students practise the dialogues, while the third student listens and monitors. The listener should count the number of phrases each student uses from the book, and make a note if either student repeats a phrase. Swap roles so each student has a chance to be the customer, assistant, and listener.

**Feedback:** find out which pair used the most phrases / least repetitions from the book.

## Can you remember ...?

You can use these sections before or after the **Speak out**, or as revision prompts.

# Speak out

**1** Students have the opportunity here to practise question forms in the context of clothes. Elicit a few examples from the class, or ask students one or two questions to demonstrate. Check vocabulary.

## Alternative

For a weaker class, you may want to create a class list of questions and write them on the board. In this case, make sure that there is a good number (at least 12 to 15). Students then choose five for themselves and proceed as in the Classbook. Alternatively, you could divide the class into As and Bs and split the questions between them. They can then ask and answer in A / B pairs.

**2** Students write answers to their own questions so that they have something to discuss in exercise 3. Go round and check the questions and answers, helping where necessary.

**3** Students get into pairs or groups of three and ask each other their questions. They can then see whose ideas are the most similar to theirs. Monitor and note any useful errors to discuss afterwards. You can use the **Can you remember ...?** box to check students' memory of vocabulary and phrases.

## Alternative

You may want to do this as a mingling activity. Students can continue to ask different people their questions until they find someone whose answers are the same as theirs.

**Feedback:** find out who has similar ideas about clothes and shopping in the class. This can lead into a class discussion.

---

**Don't forget**

Practice exercises, Classbook, *p.103*

Teacher's Resource Pack activity 24a, *MY WARDROBE*

Teacher's Resource Pack activity 24b, *CLOTHES QUIZ*

## 01

**1** 1 bake  run  see  use  watch
   2 cloudy  cold  cool  hot  windy
   3 question  queue  quick  quiet
     quite
   4 stadium  stamp  stand  star
     start
   5 great  greedy  Greek  green
     grey

**2** What's your first name?
   What's your surname?
   How do you spell that?

**3**
| Becky | W | Sean | M |
|---|---|---|---|
| Liam | M | Russell | M |
| Sharon | W | Greg | M |
| Ruth | W | Penny | W |
| Duncan | M | Heather | W |

**4** 1 September
   2 May
   3 three (September, November,
     December)
   4 February, every four years
   5 three (January, June, July)
   6 students' answers
   7 Christmas Day 25 December
     Valentine's Day 14 February
     New Year's Day 1 January
   8 **students' answer**
   9 **students' answer**
   10 **students' answer**

**5** 20° temperature
| 30 mph | speed |
|---|---|
| 0191 556 2233 | telephone number |
| 6758 4521 6666 9988 | credit card number |
| 30/6/99 | date |
| OX7 2PP | postcode |
| £4.99 | price |
| 1821 | year |
| 15A | bus number |

**6** 1 What's the speed limit in your
     country?
   2 How much is a large cappuccino?
   3 What's the weather like at the
     moment?
   4 What's the code for China?
   5 What's the flight number?

**7** 2 $1.50.
   5 VA0198.
   4 Hold on … it's 00 86.
   1 120 kph, but a lot of people drive
     faster.
   3 It's been very hot, over 40° last week.

**8** **students' answers**

## 02

**1** 1 Spain
   2 Japan
   3 Germany
   4 Brazil
   5 Ireland
   6 Sweden
   7 the United States
   8 France
   9 Italy
   10 China
   11 Australia
   12 the Netherlands

**2**
| -ish | Spanish |
|---|---|
| | Irish |
| | Swedish |
| -an / -ian | German |
| | Brazilian |
| | American |
| | Italian |
| | Australian |
| -ese | Japanese |
| | Chinese |
| other | French |
| | Dutch |

**3** 1 Where **was** James yesterday?
     He was in London.
   2 Who**'s** that woman over there?
     She's the new personnel manager.
   3 **Are** John and Alice at school?
     No, they're visiting their
     grandparents.
   4 **Are** you from the States?
     No, I'm Canadian.
   5 What**'s** his job?
     He's an accountant.
   6 Where**'s** Karen?
     She's on holiday.
   7 **Is** Sam coming to the cinema?
     No, he isn't, he's busy this evening.
   8 How **are** your parents?
     They're fine.
   9 **Were** you on holiday last week?
     No, I was off sick.
   10 **Am** I late?
     Only five minutes.

**4** 1 A Where is Marzia from?
     B She's from Parma, in Italy.
   2 A What is her job?
     B She's a nurse (in an old people's
       home).
   3 A What is her pay like?
     B (It's) terrible.
   4 A Where was Jim last year?
     B (He was) in Parma.
   5 A Who was he with?
     B (He was with) his wife.

   6 A What was the weather like?
     B (It was) rainy and misty.
   7 A What was the food like?
     B (It was) wonderful.
   8 A When were they there before?
     B (They were there) two years ago.

**5** 1 No, they aren't, they're in South
     America.
   2 No, **it isn't / it's not**, it's the capital of
     Kenya.
   3 No, **he wasn't**, he was one of the
     Beatles.
   4 No, **he wasn't**, he was Austrian.
   5 No, **they aren't / they're not**, they're
     mammals.
   6 No, **they weren't**, they were in
     Poland.
   7 No, **it isn't**, it's Elizabeth.
   8 **students' answer**

**6** 1 It was foggy yesterday.
   2 **She** was in hospital last month.
   3 **It** is for sale.
   4 **They** were here yesterday.
   5 **He** is a businessman.
   6 **We** are going shopping.

## 03

**1**

| | |
|---|---|
| Mark | husband |
| Michael | nephew |
| Holly | mother |
| Maria | sister-in-law |
| Jane | grandmother |
| Stanley | grandson |
| Justin | brother |
| Bernie | father |
| John | grandfather |
| Janet | daughter |
| Harry | son |
| Sally | granddaughter |

**2**
1 I've got one brother.
2 My grandfather's name is **John**.
3 I've got **two** children.
4 My daughter **hasn't got / doesn't have any** children.
   *or* My **son** has got two children.
5 I've got **one** nephew.
6 My sister-in-law is called **Maria**.
7 Stanley is my **grandson**.
   *or* **Sally** is my granddaughter.
8 Harry's sister is called **Janet**.

**3**
1 She's got fair hair.
2 They**'ve got** two children.
3 I can't come. I **haven't got** a ticket.
4 A  Where's the TV guide?
   B  I think Ben**'s got** it upstairs.
5 Can I borrow a fiver? I **haven't got** any money.
6 I love Edinburgh. It**'s got** just about everything you need.
7 Mary**'s got** a toothache.
8 Mr and Mrs Davies **have got** a new Mercedes.
9 The bookshop across the road **has got** the best selection of books I know.
10 He **hasn't got** a car. He can't afford it.

**4**
1 Have you got any change?
2 Have you got any brothers and sisters?
3 Have you got a mobile?
4 Have you got any plans for the weekend?
5 Have you got a light?
6 Have you got a big family?
+ students' answers

**5**
1 building
2 floor
3 living room
4 watching
5 reading
6 dining room
7 bedrooms
8 balcony

**6**

| | |
|---|---|
| bathroom | soap |
| | towels |
| | toilet paper |
| bedroom | wardrobe |
| | duvet |
| | pillow |
| living room | hi-fi |
| | bookcase |
| | coffee table |
| kitchen | dishwasher |
| | pots and pans |
| | washing-up liquid |

## British and American English

**1**

| British spelling | American spelling |
|---|---|
| favourite | favorite |
| theatre | theater |
| centre | center |
| colour | color |

**2**

| British English | American English |
|---|---|
| flat | apartment |
| lift | elevator |
| boot | trunk |
| fizzy drink | soda |
| motorway | highway |

## Reading

| | |
|---|---|
| a house in the suburbs | 2, 4 |
| a flat in the city centre | 1, 5 |
| a house in a small village | 3, 6 |

## Writing

students' answers

## Test your spelling

| | |
|---|---|
| daughter | favourite |
| surname | forty |
| terrible | businessman |
| tomorrow | fifteen |
| niece | grandfather |

## 04

**1**
| | | | |
|---|---|---|---|
| 1 | have | 4 | visit |
| 2 | go | 5 | read |
| 3 | watch | | |

**2**
I have a cocktail before dinner.                           A
I drive to work – I get there at about 8.30.               B
I play tennis with friends in the afternoon.               A
I don't have a lunch break – just coffee in the office.    B
I get home at around 8.00 in the evening.                  B
I get up at 6.30 in the morning.                           B
I get up at about 10.00.                                   A
I have breakfast by the pool.                              A

**3**  A
I get up at about 10.00.
I have breakfast by the pool.
I play tennis with friends in the afternoon.
I have a cocktail before dinner.
B
I get up at 6.30 in the morning.
I drive to work – I get there at about 8.30.
I don't have a lunch break – just coffee in the office.
I get home at around 8.00 in the evening.

**4**  students' answers

**5**
| | | | |
|---|---|---|---|
| 1 | speaks | 6 | changes |
| 2 | drinks / has | 7 | move |
| 3 | opens | 8 | meets |
| 4 | watch | 9 | smokes |
| 5 | have | 10 | live |

**6**
1 Simon speaks French but he doesn't speak Russian.
2 My mother drinks tea but she doesn't drink coffee.
3 The National Museum opens from Monday to Saturday but it doesn't open on Sunday.
4 They watch videos but they don't go to the cinema.
5 I have toast for breakfast, but I don't have cereal.

**7**
1 What languages does Simon speak?
2 How much tea does your mother drink?
3 When does the National Museum open?
4 Do they go to the cinema?
5 What do you have for breakfast?

**8**  students' answers

**9**
1 10.50
2 BA967
3 two
4 23.30
5 BA965
6 Mondays, Wednesdays, Fridays

## Writing

students' answers

## 05

1. 1 ✗
   2 ✓
   3 ✓
   4 ✗
   5 ✓
   6 ✗

2. 1 pushes
   2 goes
   3 finishes
   4 teaches
   5 watches (not in the letter)
   6 studies

3. 1 watches
   2 studies
   3 goes
   4 finishes
   5 boxes
   6 passes

4. What time?   Nine o'clock.
   Where?   In leaf hut classrooms.
   Who?   A local family.
   How often?   Once a year.
   What?   Fish, rice, and sweet potato.
   Why?   Because there aren't enough chairs and desks.

5. 1 What time does Becky start work?
   2 Where does she teach?
   3 Who does she live with?
   4 How often does Ruth see her friends?
   5 What is Becky bored with?
     *or* What does Becky eat?
   6 Why do Becky's students sit three or four to a desk?

6. 1 The bus is often early.
   2 Janice often finishes work early.
   3 I sometimes just sit and do nothing.
   4 He hardly ever watches TV.
   5 Mark never does the washing-up.
   6 What time do you usually get up?
   7 We don't always eat meat.
   8 They're often late.

7. 1 e
   2 f
   3 b
   4 a
   5 d
   6 c

8. students' answers

## 06

1. solicitor
   decorator
   farmer
   sailor
   writer
   actor
   waiter
   plumber
   translator
   bank manager

2. I'm an au pair. I work for a family in America.
   I'm a businesswoman. I work for a multinational company / in an office in the centre of town.
   I'm a computer programmer. I work for a multinational company / in a computer lab in the university / in an office in the centre of town.
   I'm a doctor. I work in a children's hospital.
   I'm a secretary. I work for a multinational company / in an office in the centre of town.
   I'm a teacher. I work in a school near here.
   I'm a lawyer. I work for a multinational company / in an office in the centre of town.
   I'm an architect. I work for a multinational company / in an office in the centre of town.

3. 1 doctor
   2 electrician
   3 architect
   4 builder
   5 plumber
   6 mechanic
   7 vet
   8 babysitter
   9 decorator
   10 dentist
   The word down the middle is *occupation*.

4. students' answers

5. 1 Applicants
   2 experience
   3 a degree
   4 essential
   5 motivated
   6 skills
   7 salary
   8 details

## Test your spelling

1 breakfast
2 doesn't
3 colleagues
4 temperature
5 salary

## Reading

| | | | |
|---|---|---|---|
| 1 | b | 5 | a |
| 2 | a | 6 | b |
| 3 | b | 7 | a |
| 4 | b | 8 | a |

## 07

1. 1 hiking
   2 canoeing
   3 rafting
   4 horse-riding
   5 biking
   6 city sightseeing

2. students' answers

3. students' answers

4. possible answers
   She really likes travelling.
   She's interested in South America.
   She enjoys going to the cinema.
   She likes (listening to) music.
   She's interested in learning Italian.

5. students' answers

6. 1 He likes going to the gym.
   2 They enjoy going to the cinema.
   3 Mary loves gardening.
   4 John loves driving.
   5 We hate (playing) computer games.
   6 George enjoys spending time with his children.
   7 I can't stand getting up early.
   8 I don't mind (going to) the dentist.

7. driving
   taking
   getting
   hoping
   watching
   cycling
   teaching
   studying

## 08

1 students' answers

2 students' answers

3 students' answers

4 students' answers

5  1 What's **on** at the cinema this week?

   2 The bus stops right **outside / opposite / next to / near** the theatre.

   3 The restaurant's **on / in** Grindlay Street.

   4 We're going out to eat **at** that restaurant **on** Saturday evening.

   5 We're taking my parents **to** an art gallery.

   6 **A** How are you getting home?
      **B** **By** taxi, probably.

   7 Can you book tickets **by** phone?

   8 On Sundays you can get **in** free.

6  1 The cinema has an **international** film festival.

   2 This **friendly** restaurant has a **creative** menu.

   3 This **old-fashioned** café has the **best** waiters in town.

   4 The **beautiful** city park accommodates an **excellent** zoo.

   5 The standard **opening** hours for **all** museums are 10 a.m.–6 p.m. in summer.

   6 Vienna has about 150 **art galleries**, most **of them** in the city centre.

   7 This wine bar has **live** music – jazz **on Mondays**, blues on Fridays.

   8 Club 66 is **open** till 6.00 a.m. on Saturdays and **Sundays**.

   9 The theatre is very **glamorous** and is still the home of Austrian **drama**.

## Reading

1 Where is it?

2 What's the phone number?

3 What's the website (address)?

4 How much is admission?
   *or* How much does it cost to get in?

5 What time does it close on Fridays and Saturdays?

6 Where's the restaurant?

## 09

1

```
u p c h i p s h o p o t k
u k g w g l r e p b l a p
n v b b m w o b k m d z h
d v k r s u i p b j k b
e n c i u h n c q u r a o
r t h d t o d k l s k j e
g b e g c e a p r s e a q
r u m e o s b m b t k m h
o b i q w h o v u o o f d
u b s j t o u a k p a r k
n n t x h p t p q x n j z
d m s p o s t o f f i c e
r t r a i n s t a t i o n
```

2  1 stadium

   2 ice-rink

   3 square

   4 mall

   5 port

2 an indoor area for skating

4 a covered shopping centre

5 a place for ships, boats, and ferries

1 an area for games and competitions …

3 an open area with four sides …

## Writing

students' answers

## British and American English

1 *mall* is American

2  liquor store     off-licence
   rest room     public toilet
   drugstore     chemist's
   the subway     the underground
   gas station     petrol station
   apartment building     block of flats
   parking lot     car park
   store     shop

3  1 Could you tell me where the museum is, please?

   2 Is there a Chinese restaurant near here?

   3 Is this the way to the Italian restaurant?

   4 Do you know if there's a chemist's near here?

4  **Is there**
    a newsagent near here?
    a public convenience near here?

   **Could you tell me**
    if there's a park near here?
    where the railway station is, please?
    the way to the police station?

   **Is**
    this the way to the library?
    the stadium near here?

   **Do you know**
    if there's a park near here?
    where the railway station is, please?
    the way to the police station?

   **I'm looking**
    for a book shop.

   **How do I get to**
    the shopping centre?

5  1 a
   2 c
   3 e
   4 d
   5 b
   6 f

## Test your spelling

shopping     restaurant
traffic     museum
between     tourist
practising     opposite
admission     art gallery

## 10

**1** 5 I thought the orchestra would be much better.
2 Not the best I've had, but not the worst.
3 That's the last time I eat there.
6 Lots of paintings, but none of them much good.
4 I'd like to read something else by her.
1 I'm going to see it again tomorrow.

**3** students' answers

**4** students' answers

## 11

**1** 1 're visiting
2 isn't coming
3 Are you flying
4 is having
5 **are coming**
6 's having
7 is driving
8 are playing

**2** students' answers

**3** 1 What are you doing at the weekend / this weekend?
2 Who are you going with?
3 How are you getting there?
4 Where are you staying?
5 Why are you asking?

**4** in December
the afternoon
early April
late September
on Tuesday
17 November
Wednesday morning
Saturday evening
at the weekend
8.30 in the evening
midnight
4.30

**5** students' answers

**6** Tony What are you doing tonight?
Mike I'm going out with Rebecca.
Ally Where are you going?
Mike We're meeting Louise and Andrew at Umberto's. It's a great restaurant. The food's excellent.
Tony Mary is coming up from London tonight. Can we join you? I know she loves Italian food.
Mike Yes, sure. We're leaving here at 8.00. What about you, Ally, are you doing anything?
Ally No, I'm staying in. I'm not feeling very well.
Tony Why? What's wrong?
Ally I've got a splitting headache. But thanks for asking, anyway.

## 12

**1** 1 This is a platform alteration. Would all passengers waiting on platform 3 for the 8.45 to Cambridge please go to platform 1?
2 We apologize for the late arrival of the 12.15 from Manchester. It is currently 5 minutes late, and is due to arrive at 15.30.
3 This is a change of gate. Flight BA0192 to Paris is now boarding at gate 9.
4 All Air France flights leave from terminal two.

**2** students' answers

### Reading

1 The zoo has more buses – there are six.
2 Opposite the Palace.
3 15 minutes.
4 Three miles.
5 Yes.
6 01383 621249.
7 No.
8 No, it's free.

### Writing

**1** 1 travel
2 around
3 service
4 Getting
5 plenty
6 expensive
7 transport
8 few

**2** students' answers

**3** students' answers

### Test your spelling

1 exhibition    disappointing
2 absolutely    brilliant
3 accommodation    holiday
4 dinner    Wednesday
5 Buses    comfortable

## 13

**1**
  1  I'm **standing** outside the post office.

  2  I'm **having** lunch in Billie's Bistro.

  3  I'm **walking** down the High Street. I'm just passing the library.

  4  I'm **sitting** on a bench in the park.

**2**  students' answers

**3**  students' answers

**4**
  1  Great to hear from you after so long.

  2  I hope your new job's going well.

  3  You won't believe it, but I've got a new job too!

  4  I'm working with my brother in his shop.

  5  He needs help and I need the money!

  6  I'm only working at weekends because I want to study during the week.

  7  I finish college this summer, so then I can a real job.

## 14

**1**
  1  Is that Julia?

  2  Yes, speaking.

  3  It's Michael here.

  4  Is Robert there?

  5  Can I take a message?

  6  Can he phone me back before 9.00 tonight?

  7  OK, just let me get a pen.

  8  What number can he call you on?

**2**
  1  address book

  2  phone book

  3  phone box

  4  address

  5  postbox

**3**
  1  alarm

  2  time

  3  clock

  4  morning

  5  called

  6  evening

  7  enter

  8  rings

  9  answer

  10  second

## Reading

**1**
  1  999.

  2  112.

  3  Ambulance.

  4  Coastguard.

**2**
  1  Where's the problem / trouble?

  2  What's the problem / trouble?

  3  Where are you calling from?

## Writing

students' answers

## 15

**1**
  4  You should take it back to the shop.

  3  You should go to the police.

  5  You should take her to the doctor.

  2  You should fly.

  6  You shouldn't spend so much!

  1  You should try putting a new battery in it.

**2**  students' answers

**3**  students' answers

## Test your spelling

| | |
|---|---|
| library | worried |
| difficult | excited |
| computer | afternoon |
| address | headache |
| message | travelling |

## 16

**1**
1. cauliflower
2. onions
3. oranges
4. cabbage
5. grapes
6. apples
7. avocado
8. bananas
9. plums
10. peas
11. beans
12. carrots

**2** students' answers

**3** students' answers

**4**
5. When you first arrive in the restaurant.
2. Before you look at the menu.
1. After you look at the menu.
4. After you finish ordering your starter and your main course.
6. After you finish eating your main course.
3. After your meal.

**5**
3. Yes, please, black.
1. Not quite.
2. Yes, I'll have mineral water, please.
2 / 3 / 4 / 6. Not for me, thanks.
1 / 4. Um, yes … a green salad, please.
5. Smoking, please.
1. Yes, we are.
3 / 4 / 6. No, thanks, can we just have the bill, please?

**6**
Could I have   the menu?
      more wine?
      a bottle of water?
      the bill?

**7**
| | | | |
|---|---|---|---|
| furniture | U | hair | U |
| information | U | luggage | U |
| money | U | news | U |
| problem | C | advice | U |

**8**
1. isn't
2. is
3. is
4. feels
5. isn't
6. doesn't grow

**9** students' answers

## Reading

**1**
1. ✓   4. ✗
2. ✗   5. ✗
3. ✗   6. ✓

**2**
| | |
|---|---|
| high | prices |
| private | cafés and restaurants |
| traditional | Russian restaurants |
| energetic | dancing |
| loud | music |
| affordable | restaurants |

**3** students' answers

## 17

**1**
1. a knife
2. a fork
3. a wine glass
4. a bottle
5. salt and pepper
6. a spoon
7. chopsticks
8. a jug
9. the bill

**2** possible answer

Waiter   Hello, the Star of India.
Customer   Hello, I'd like to book a table, please.
or Hello, I'd like to make a reservation, please.
Waiter   When would that be for?
Customer   This evening, at 8.00.
Waiter   For how many?
Customer   Four.
Waiter   Yes, that will be fine. Could I take a name and phone number?
Customer   Florio. My phone number's 866 4545.
Waiter   Thank you. We'll see you then.

## 18

**1**
1. What film did Vic and Sarah see?
2. Did they like it?
3. Where did they meet Alison?
4. What did Bruce cook?
5. What did Alison give Vic?
6. Why did Alison give Vic a CD?
7. What time did Karen leave Bruce's?
8. What was the fish pie like?

**2** across
| | | | | |
|---|---|---|---|---|
| 1 | rang | 14 | did | |
| 4 | understood | 15 | lost | |
| 7 | began | 18 | cost | |
| 9 | ate | 20 | knew | |
| 11 | taught | 22 | wore | |

down
| | | | | |
|---|---|---|---|---|
| 1 | ran | 12 | ago | |
| 2 | hit | 13 | got | |
| 3 | found | 14 | drank | |
| 5 | drove | 16 | spoke | |
| 6 | heard | 17 | flew | |
| 7 | bought | 19 | told | |
| 8 | gave | 21 | won | |
| 10 | wrote | | | |

*ago* (12 down) isn't a past simple verb

**3** students' answers

**4**
| | | | |
|---|---|---|---|
| 1 | chose | 8 | didn't think |
| 2 | liked | 9 | hated |
| 3 | reminded | 10 | left |
| 4 | went | 11 | upset |
| 5 | went | 12 | paid |
| 6 | was | 13 | phoned |
| 7 | took | 14 | got |

## Writing

students' answers

**5**
| | |
|---|---|
| opened | remembered |
| | closed |
| | listened |
| | changed |
| | loved |
| finished | cooked |
| | booked |
| | danced |
| | liked |
| | looked |
| started | repeated |
| | ended |

**6** students' answers

**7**
| | | |
|---|---|---|
| 3–0 | football score | nil |
| 0% | interest rates | nought |
| 0º | temperature | zero |
| 305 7088 | telephone number | oh |

**8** students' answers

## Test your spelling

| | |
|---|---|
| pizza | clothes |
| vegetables | pepper |
| fridge | sandwich |
| expensive | birthday |

## 19

**1** possible answers
1 Travelling by train is better than by bus because …
2 I like evenings better than mornings because …
3 I feel more comfortable in jeans than in a suit because …
4 Living in the city is better than living in the country because …
5 Living in a flat is more convenient than living in a house because …
6 Being a student is easier than working because …

**2** students' answers

**3**
1 ✓
2 ✗
3 ✗
4 ✓
5 ✓
6 ✓
7 ✗
8 ✗

**4** students' answers

## 20

**1**
| | |
|---|---|
| check-in | economy class |
| boarding pass | business class |
| first class | departure lounge |
| single | gate |
| arrival hall | passport control |
| round trip | baggage reclaim |

**2**
3 Return, please.
5 3969 7854 3555 3212.
1 Two adults and two children.
4 Credit card, please.
6 August 2007.
2 Next Saturday.

# Reading

**1**
1 £610.
2
| | |
|---|---|
| you lose your passport | £500 |
| your plane is delayed | £300 |
| you need an ambulance | £20,000 |
| there is a plane crash | £200,000 |
| you have to go to hospital | £10,000 |

**2**
1 ✗
2 ✗
3 ?
4 ✓
5 ✓
6 ✗
7 ✓
8 ?
9 ?
10 ✓

**3**
| regular | irregular |
|---|---|
| realize / realized | fall / fell |
| need / needed | hit / hit |
| decide / decided | be / was |
| want / wanted | get / got |
| arrive / arrived | fly / flew |
| recover / recovered | tell / told |

**4**
cost
cut
hurt
put
read
upset

## 21

**1**
1 Cromwell Road
2 Alex
3 Marzia
4 Phenecia
5 Eleni
6 Ruth
7 Vladimir
8 Alba
9 Natalie
= camper van

**2**
A Hello, York Hotel.
B Hello, **I'd like to** book a **room** for this Wednesday, please.
A Certainly, sir. What **sort / kind of** room **would you** like?
B A single with en suite **bathroom**, please.
A Yes, **we have a** single free.
B Could you tell me **how much it is / costs** ?
A It's £85.
B **Does that include** breakfast?
A Yes, it does.
B OK. Can I **phone / ring / call back** later to confirm?
A Yes, of course.

# Reading

**1**
1 Anta Hotel
2 Anta Hotel
3 Grace Hotel
4 Business and leisure guests
5 Grace Hotel
6 A sauna
7 Thai, Chinese, and international cuisine
8 Grace Hotel

**2**
| | |
|---|---|
| unfriendly | welcoming |
| indoor | outdoor |
| ugly | attractive |
| uncomfortable | comfortable |
| cold | warm |
| unknown | famous |
| local | international |

**3**
1 guest-house
2 self-catering apartment
3 camper van
4 camp-site
5 hotel

# Test your spelling
1 mountainous
2 cities
3 weather's
4 uncomfortable
5 advertisements

## 22

**1**
1 They haven't flown before.
2 Have you ever been to Edinburgh?
3 I've never won any money.
4 I haven't studied English before.
5 How many times have you met Kathryn?
6 Has she bought a car before?
7 I have been to Tokyo but Russell hasn't.
*or* Russell hasn't been to Tokyo but I have.
8 We've seen that film three times.

**2**
1 I've been
2 came
3 We have never visited
4 Have you ever seen
5 have you had
6 I saved
7 I did
8 won

**3** students' answers

**4**
1 You can **borrow** money **from** me if you need it.
2 Can I **pay by** credit card?
3 Have you got **change for** a pound?
4 Don't **lend** money **to** Jake. He never pays you back.
5 I'm **saving for** a holiday this summer, but I always seem to **spend** as fast as I earn.
6 How do you want to pay? **By cheque, by credit card**, or **in cash**?

**5** students' answers

**6** students' answers

### Reading

1 You can change money in hotels and banks.
2 The guide advises readers to buy no more local currency than necessary.
3 Tourists can use credit cards in more expensive restaurants.
4 Banks sometimes charge you a large commission for changing traveller's cheques.
5 You can change money in banks on weekdays only.

## 23

**1**
1 shoe shop
2 music shop / video shop
3 stationer's
4 computer shop
5 post office / stationer's / newsagent
6 newsagent
7 chemist's / supermarket
8 clothes shop

**2** students' answers

**3** students' answers

**4**
1 Why does Nicola like Internet shopping?
2 How much does she usually spend on Christmas presents?
3 When does she prepare her shopping list?
4 How old is she?
5 Which companies does she buy from?
6 What does Nicola also like about Internet shopping?

### Writing

**1** students' answers

**2** students' answers

## 24

**1** students' answers

**2** In Britain
1 Women usually, men sometimes
2 No
3 Yes
4 Almost always, sometimes not on Fridays
5 Yes
6 Yes
7 Yes
8 No
9 Yes, usually
10 No

### Reading

1 kilt
2 dirk (a small knife)
3 sock
4 white shirt
5 jacket
6 sporran
7 tartan plaid
8 black leather shoes
9 white dress

### Writing

students' answers

### Test your spelling

| | |
|---|---|
| borrow | fleece |
| scissors | briefcase |
| appointment | backpack |
| charity | shopping |
| suit | coffee |

# OXFORD
UNIVERSITY PRESS

Great Clarendon Street, Oxford OX2 6DP

Oxford University Press is a department
of the University of Oxford. It furthers
the University's objective of excellence in
research, scholarship, and education by
publishing worldwide in

Oxford New York

Athens Auckland Bangkok Bogotá
Buenos Aires Cape Town Chennai
Dar es Salaam Delhi Florence Hong Kong
Istanbul Karachi Kolkata Kuala Lumpur
Madrid Melbourne Mexico City Mumbai
Nairobi Paris São Paulo Shanghai
Singapore Taipei Tokyo Toronto Warsaw

with associated companies in Berlin Ibadan

Oxford and Oxford English are registered
trade marks of Oxford University Press in
the UK and in certain other countries

ISBN 0 19 434097 X

Printed in Spain by Unigraf s.l.

# doves

## the last broadcast

guitar tablature vocal

Published 2002
© International Music Publications Limited
Griffin house, 161 Hammersmith Road, London, W6 8BS, England

Edited by Chris Harvey
Music arranged by Artemis Music Ltd
Art direction & design by Rick Myers
Photography by Rich Mulhearn
Folio design by Dominic Brookman

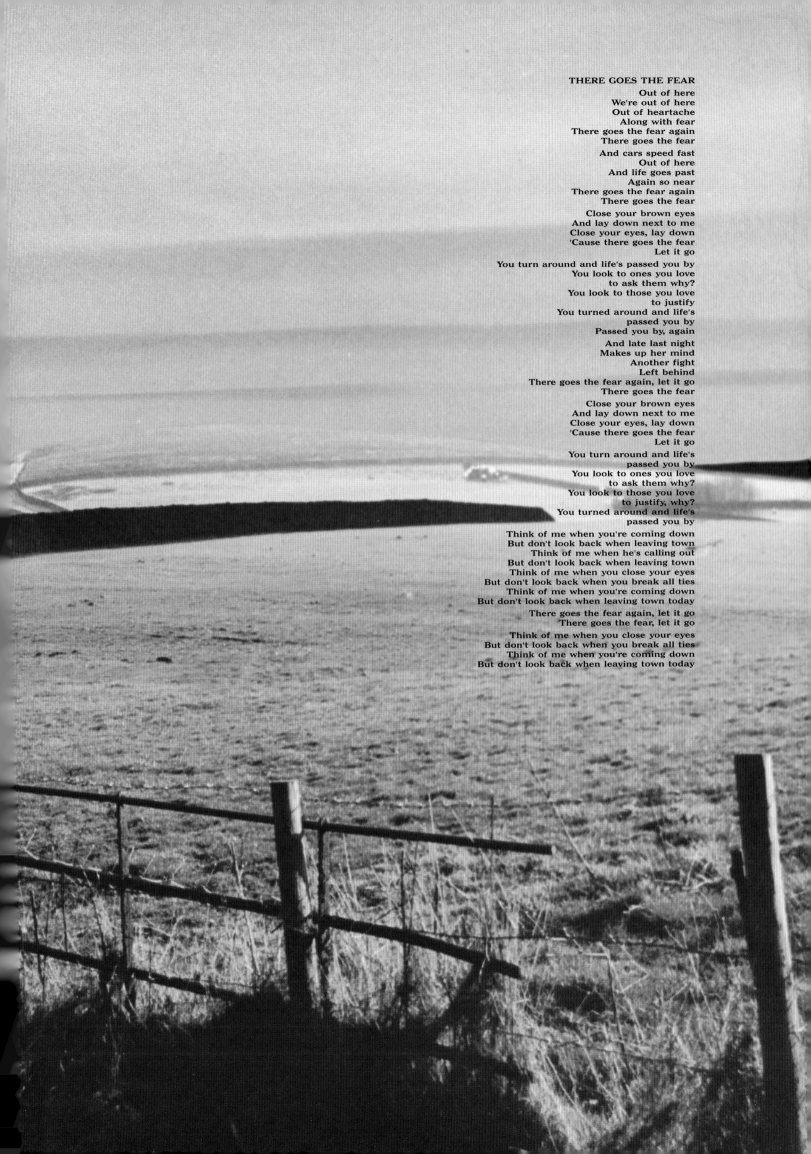

## THERE GOES THE FEAR

Out of here
We're out of here
Out of heartache
Along with fear
There goes the fear again
There goes the fear

And cars speed fast
Out of here
And life goes past
Again so near
There goes the fear again
There goes the fear

Close your brown eyes
And lay down next to me
Close your eyes, lay down
'Cause there goes the fear
Let it go

You turn around and life's passed you by
You look to ones you love
to ask them why?
You look to those you love
to justify
You turned around and life's
passed you by
Passed you by, again

And late last night
Makes up her mind
Another fight
Left behind
There goes the fear again, let it go
There goes the fear

Close your brown eyes
And lay down next to me
Close your eyes, lay down
'Cause there goes the fear
Let it go

You turn around and life's
passed you by
You look to ones you love
to ask them why?
You look to those you love
to justify, why?
You turned around and life's
passed you by

Think of me when you're coming down
But don't look back when leaving town
Think of me when he's calling out
But don't look back when leaving town
Think of me when you close your eyes
But don't look back when you break all ties
Think of me when you're coming down
But don't look back when leaving town today

There goes the fear again, let it go
There goes the fear, let it go

Think of me when you close your eyes
But don't look back when you break all ties
Think of me when you're coming down
But don't look back when leaving town today

## WORDS

Inside's a heart of summer soul
Don't let them take it away
'Cause inside something solid gold
So don't let them throw it away

Words they mean nothing
So you can't hurt me
I said words they mean nothing
So you can't stop me

I said your eyes, they say nothing
So you can't hurt me / on summer days like these
I said words they mean nothing
So you can't hurt me

Follow your own path from here
So don't listen to what they say
'Cause inside you've a heart of gold
So don't let them take this away

Words they mean nothing
So you can't hurt me / on summer days like these
I said words they mean nothing
So you can't stop me / on summer days like these

I said your eyes, they say nothing
So you can't fault me
I said words they mean nothing
So you can't hurt me

Inside a heart of pure soul
A sun rising, and falling away, like your soul
'Cause here comes something wonderful
So don't let them throw it away

Words they mean nothing
So you can't hurt me / on summer days like these
I said words they mean nothing
So you can't stop me / on summer days like these

I said your eyes, they say nothing
So you can't stop me / on summer days like these
I said words they mean nothing
So you can't hurt me

## SATELLITES

I want you to know this
My anger's all but done
Sweet Lord, I swear I've seen the darkness
Sweet Lord, I swear I've seen some pain

Satellites ahead, so hold on
Satellites I said, so come on

Here comes a strange cargo
Here comes a light that leaves out of here
Sweet Lord, all I've known is badness
Sweet Lord, all I've known is pain

Satellites ahead, so hold on
Satellites I said, so come on
For seven nights I slept, hold on
The satellites ahead, so come on

I want you to notice
My anger's all but done
And all I've known is madness

Satellites ahead, so hold on
For seven nights I slept, so come on
So hold on
So come on

## FRIDAY'S DUST

Friday's dust
Turned into a Saturdays
It wasn't meant to be this way
It wasn't meant to end so late

Friday's trust
A deal not brokered honestly
Perhaps it's just a game they played
Tell me they've not flown away

All the hope and all the wonder
All the strength that they can muster
Won't go
They won't get me down

Their desire
It seems they've got designs on me
They never want me honestly
They try to take me foolishly

All the toys and creature comforts
All the dreams that they can rupture
Won't go

Friday's dust takes all the love we own

## CAUGHT BY THE RIVER

Son, what have you done?
You're caught by the river
You're coming undone
Life you know it can't be so easy
But you can't just leave it
'Cause you're not in control no more

And you give it all away
Would you give it all away now?
Don't let it come apart
Don't want to see you come apart

Son, what are you doing?
You learned a hard lesson
When you stood by the water
You and I were so full of love and hope
Would you give it all up now?
Would you give in just to spite them all?

And you give it all away
Would you give it all away now?
Don't let it come apart
Don't want to see you come apart

'Cause you give it all away
And you give it all away now
Don't let it come apart
Don't want to see you come apart

Lay, I lay in the long grass
So many people
So many people pass
Stay, stay here and lie on back
Get down in the cornfields
Stay till we're caught at last

Give it all away
Give it all away now
Don't let it come apart
Don't want to see you come apart

And you give it all away
You give it all away now
Don't let it come apart
Don't want to see you come apart

And you give it all away

## THE SULPHUR MAN

Fate, bought you, brought you
Next to ghosts
They, talk in code
Looking for the way out
I hope, I hope
I hope you want to live a day
And learn to cope
I hope you find what matters

Through the streets and on your own
Almost lost and almost home
We'll be looking all we can
We'll be searching for the Sulphur Man

Pills stop you, stopped you feeling life
Fall into a hole
Sympathy and all
A soul in tatters
A soul as black as coal
I hope, I hope
I wish you could find what matters

Through the streets and on your own
Almost lost and almost home
We'll be looking all we can
We'll be searching for the Sulphur Man

## M62 SONG

Moonshine, I'm waiting for a love that never comes
Moonshine, wishing for a time that never was

I'm waiting for a time, for truth to call
I'm waiting for a sign, to show me all
I'm waiting for my love

Moonshine, drinking to a love that's gone on by
Moonshine, look into the stars as cars go by

I'm waiting for a time, for truth to call
I'm waiting for a sign, to show my all
I'm waiting for a love

I'm waiting for a time, for truth to call
I'm waiting for a sign, to show me all
I'm waiting for my love, waiting for a love
Waiting for my love, waiting for my love
Moonshine waiting for a love that never comes

# INTRO

**Words and Music by Williams/Goodwin/Williams**

# WORDS

**Words and Music by Williams/Goodwin/Williams**

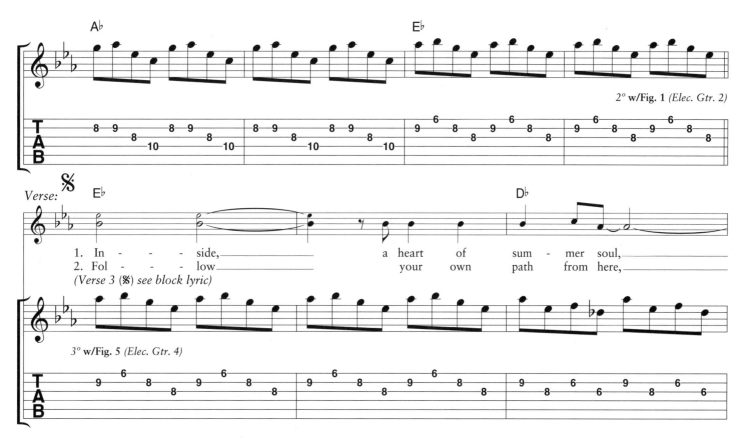

Verse:

1. In - - side,_____ a heart of sum - mer soul,_____
2. Fol - - low_____ your own path from here,_____

*(Verse 3 (%) see block lyric)*

*3° w/Fig. 5 (Elec. Gtr. 4)*

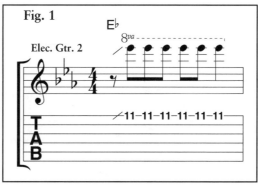

Fig. 1

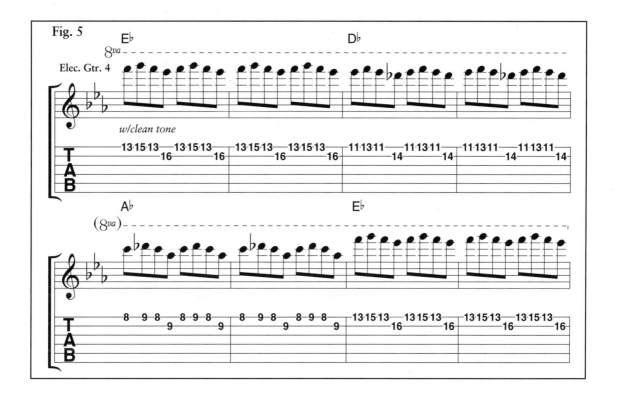

Fig. 5

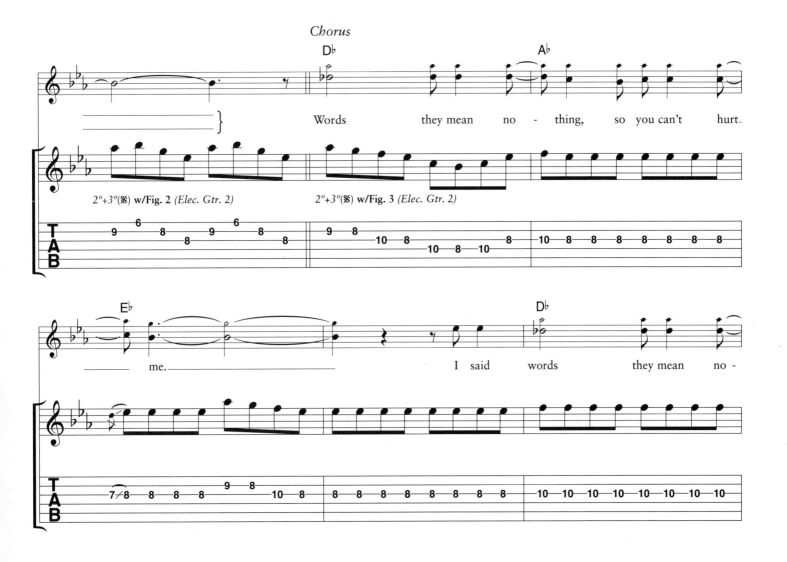

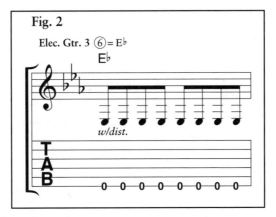

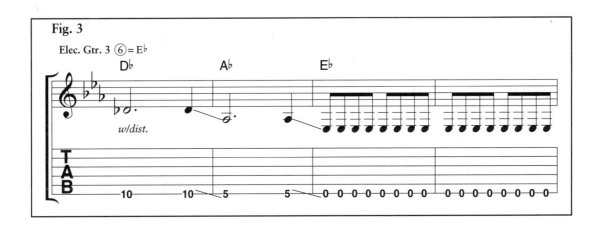

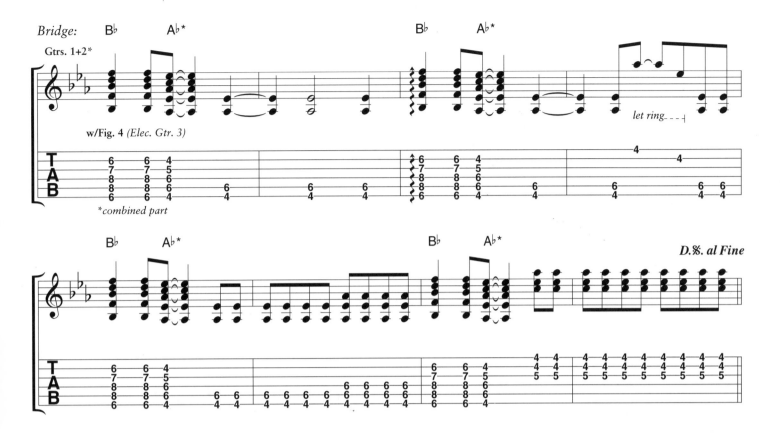

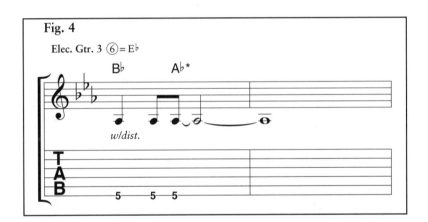

*Verse 3:*
Inside a heart of pure soul
A sun rising and falling away (like your soul)
So here comes something wonderful
So don't let them throw it away
They don't know nothing.

Words they mean nothing *etc.*

# THERE GOES THE FEAR

**Words and Music by Williams/Goodwin/Williams**

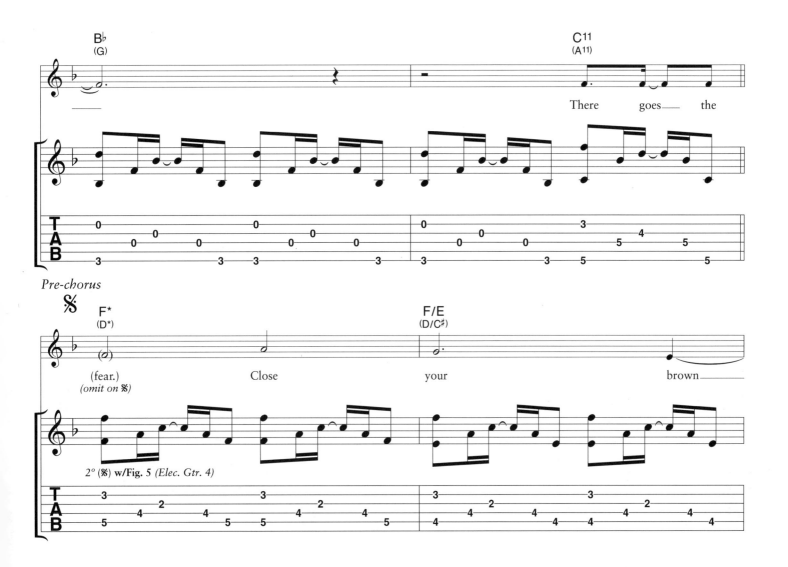

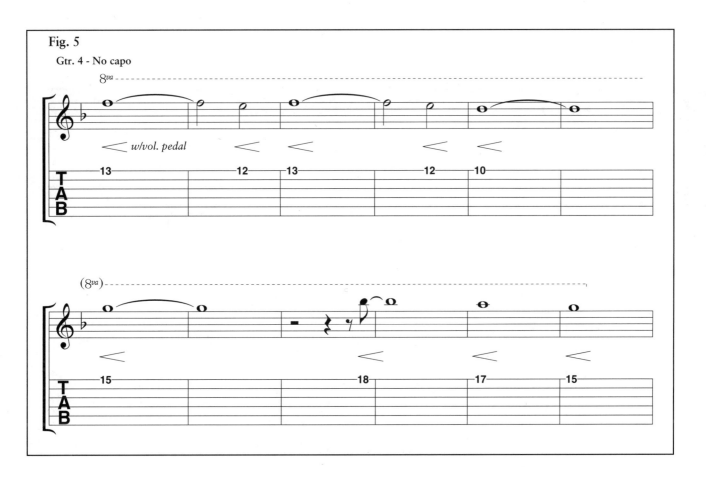

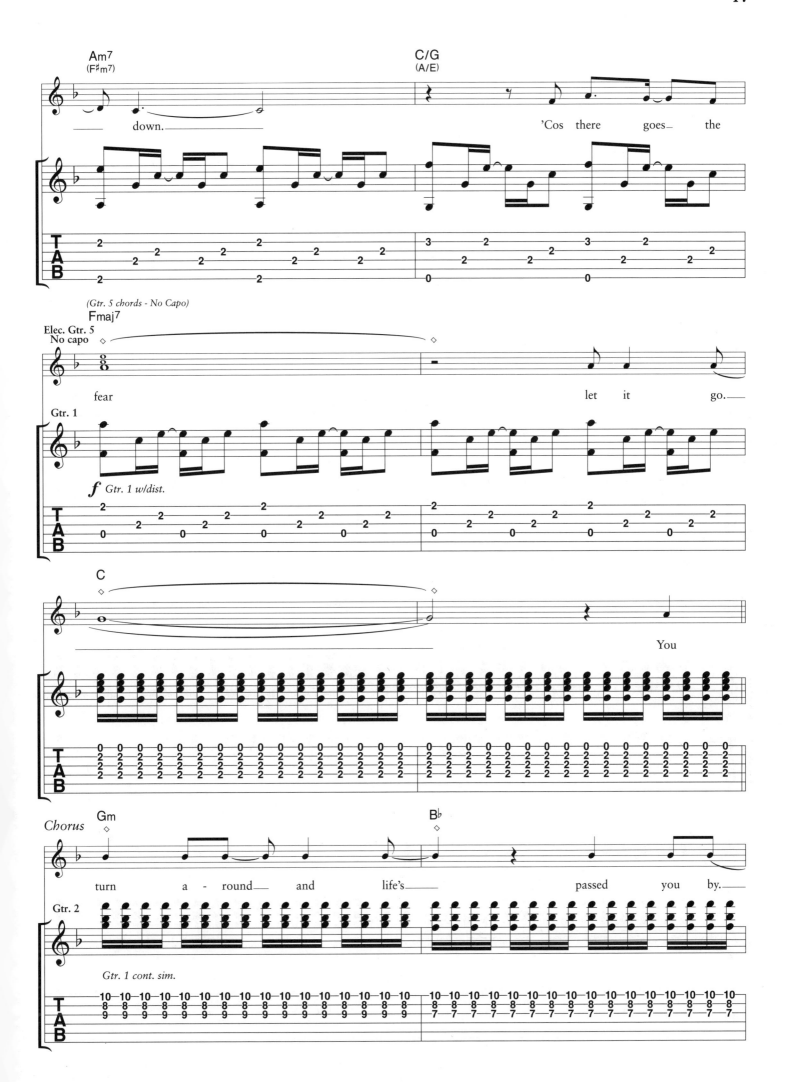

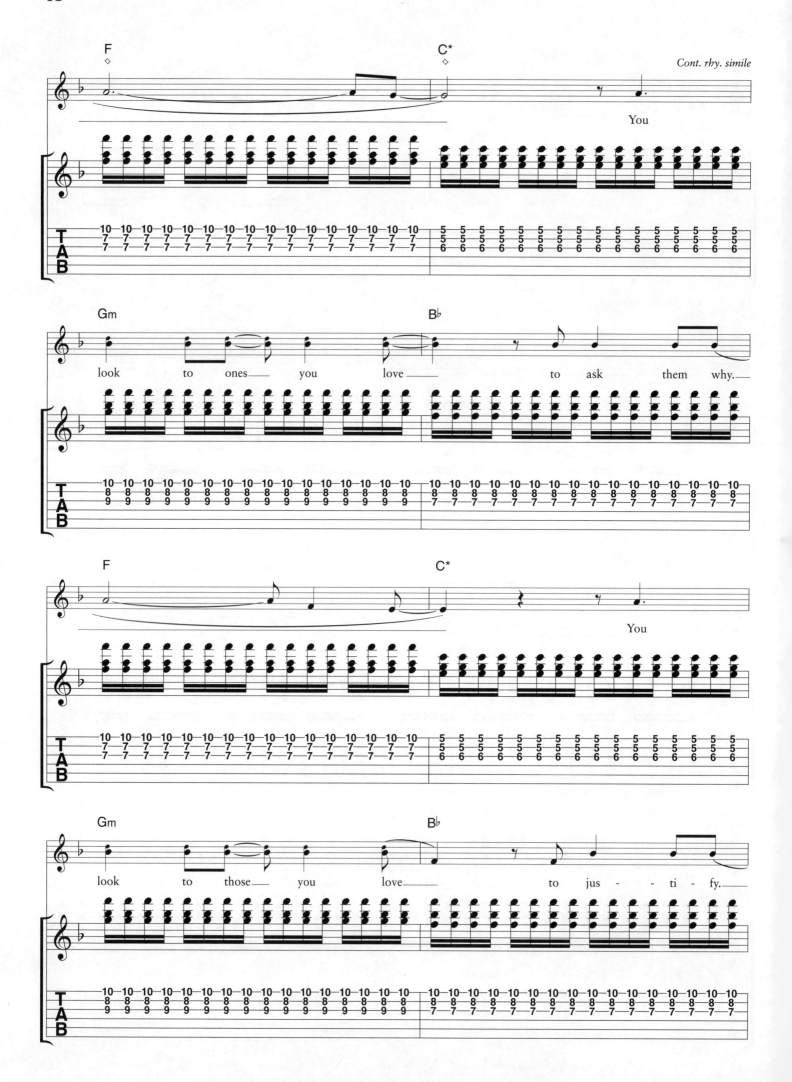

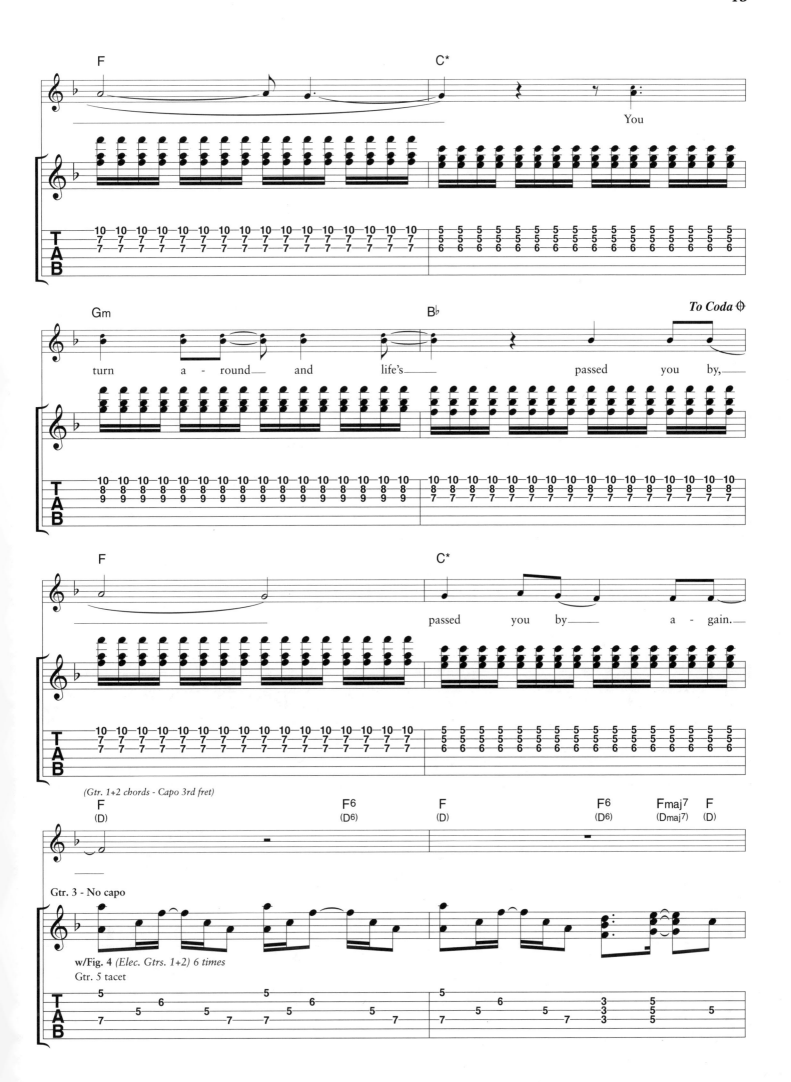

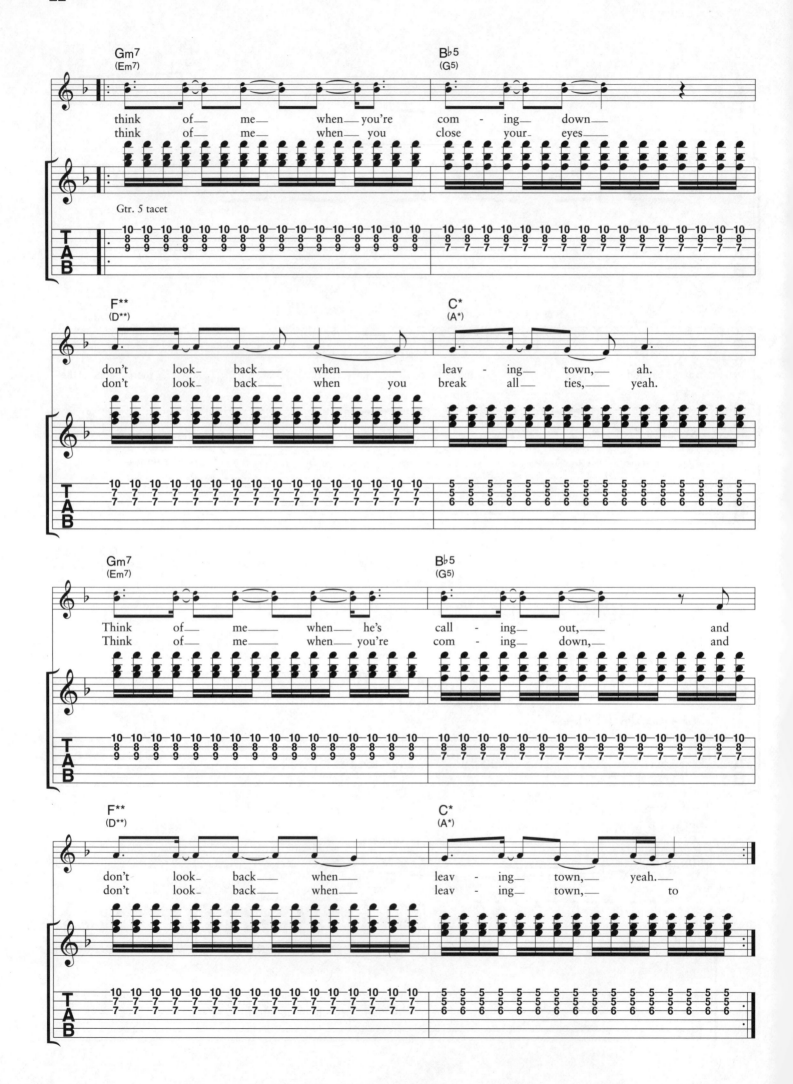

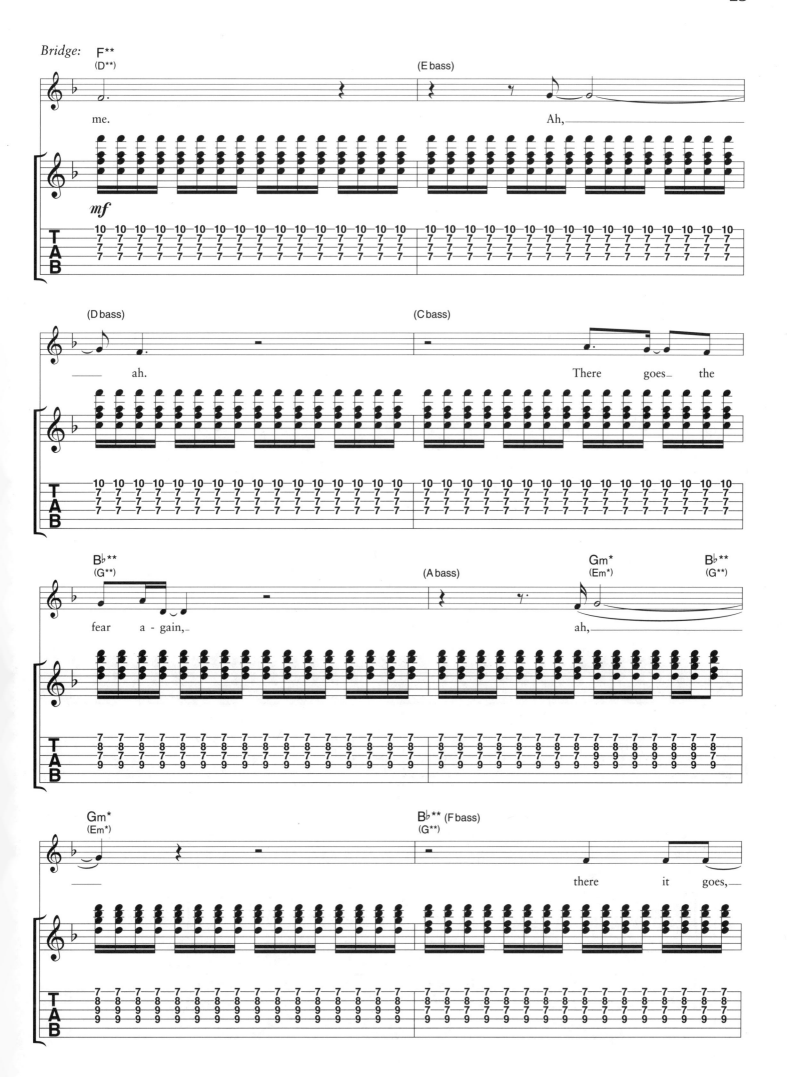

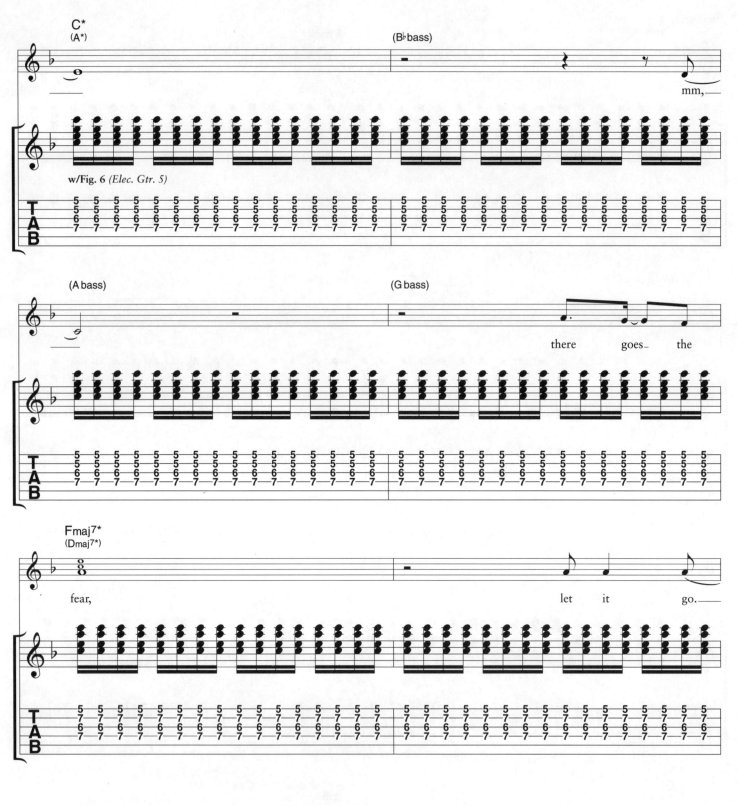

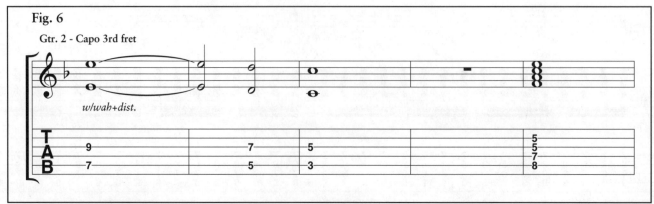

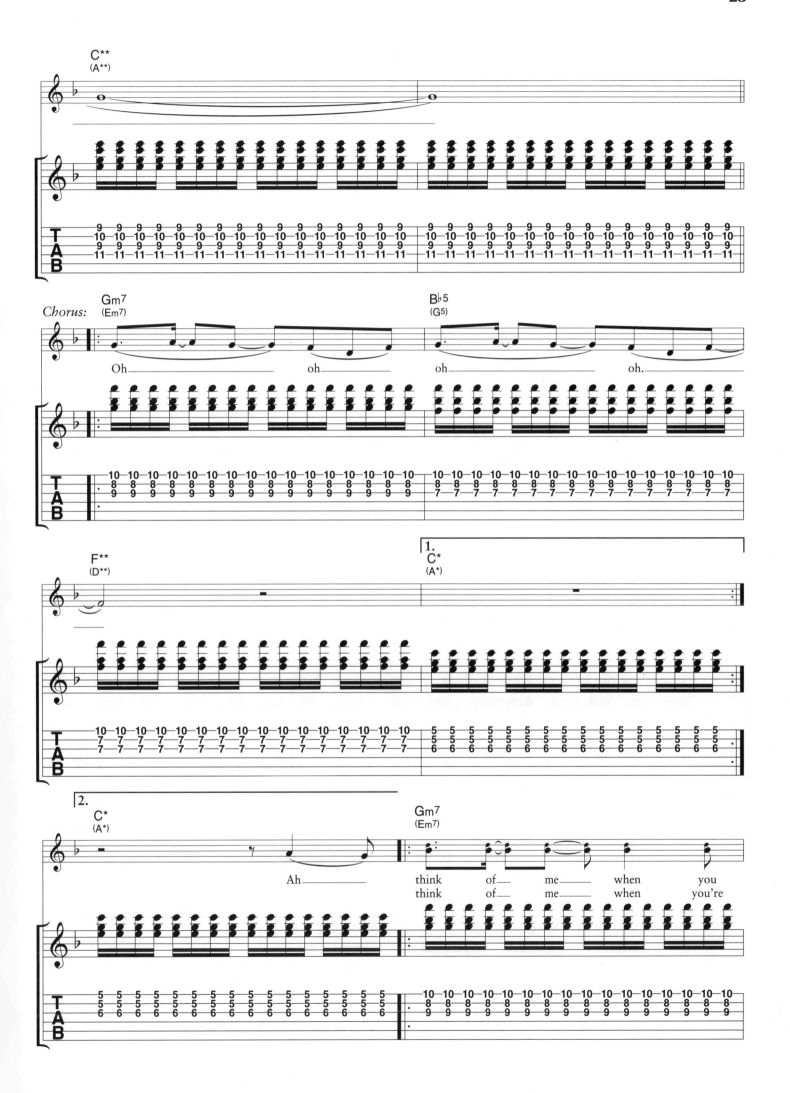

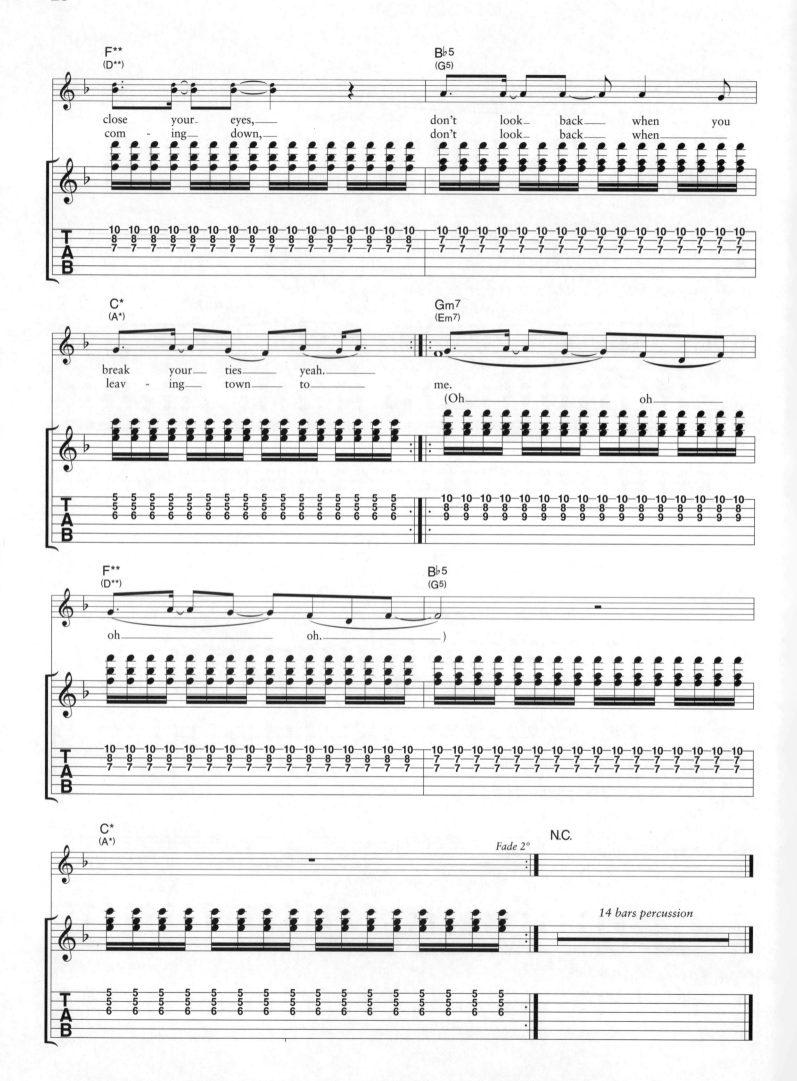

# M62 SONG

**Words and Music by**
**Williams/Goodwin/Williams/Fripp/Giles/Lake/McDonald/Sinfield**

Tune Gtr. down 1 tone

# WHERE WE'RE CALLING FROM

**Words and Music by Williams/Goodwin/Williams**

# N.Y.

**Words and Music by Williams/Goodwin/Williams**

*Verse:*

2. On the road and out of town, we're mov-ing on again. Ev-'ry-thing they say is true this

ci-ty is in-sane.___ Ev-'ry pos-si-bi-li-ty, noth-ing's left to chance.___

(They're) Throw-ing rocks and pav-ing stones, who says it has to last. On the run___

w/**Fig. 2** *(Elec. Gtr. 3)*

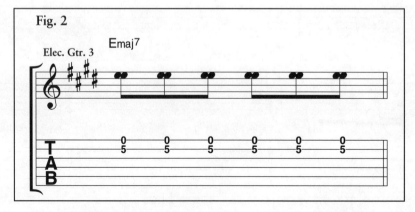

**Fig. 2**

Elec. Gtr. 3

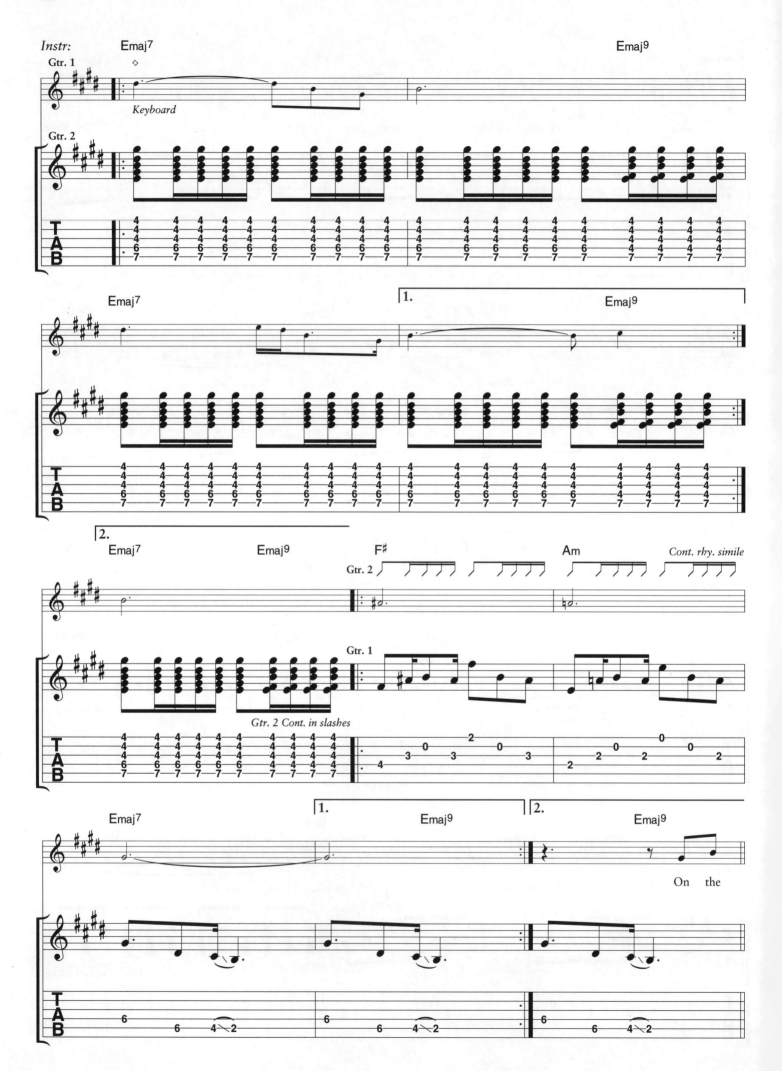

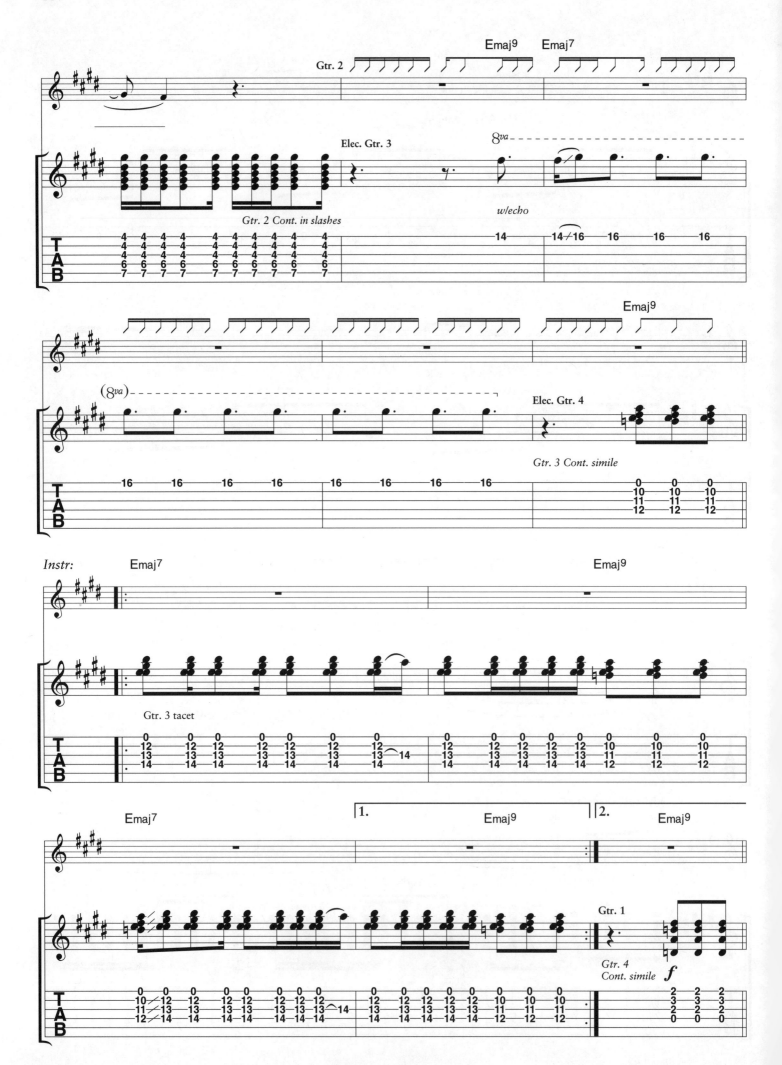

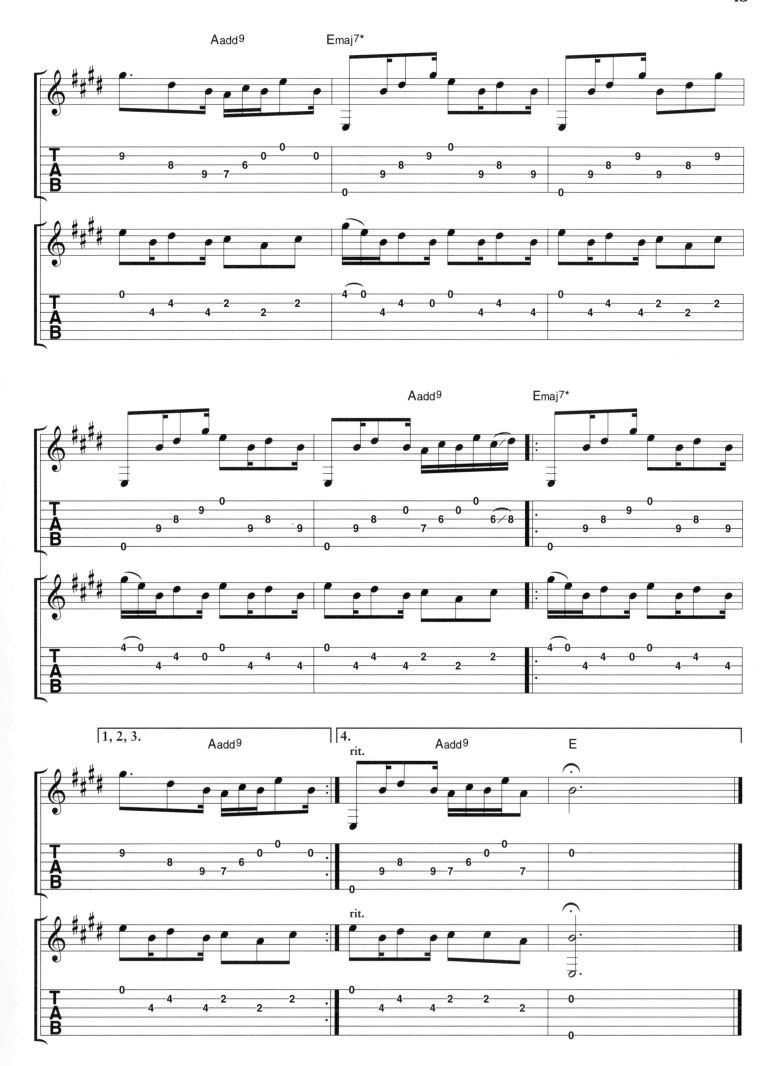

# FRIDAY'S DUST

**Words and Music by Williams/Goodwin/Williams**

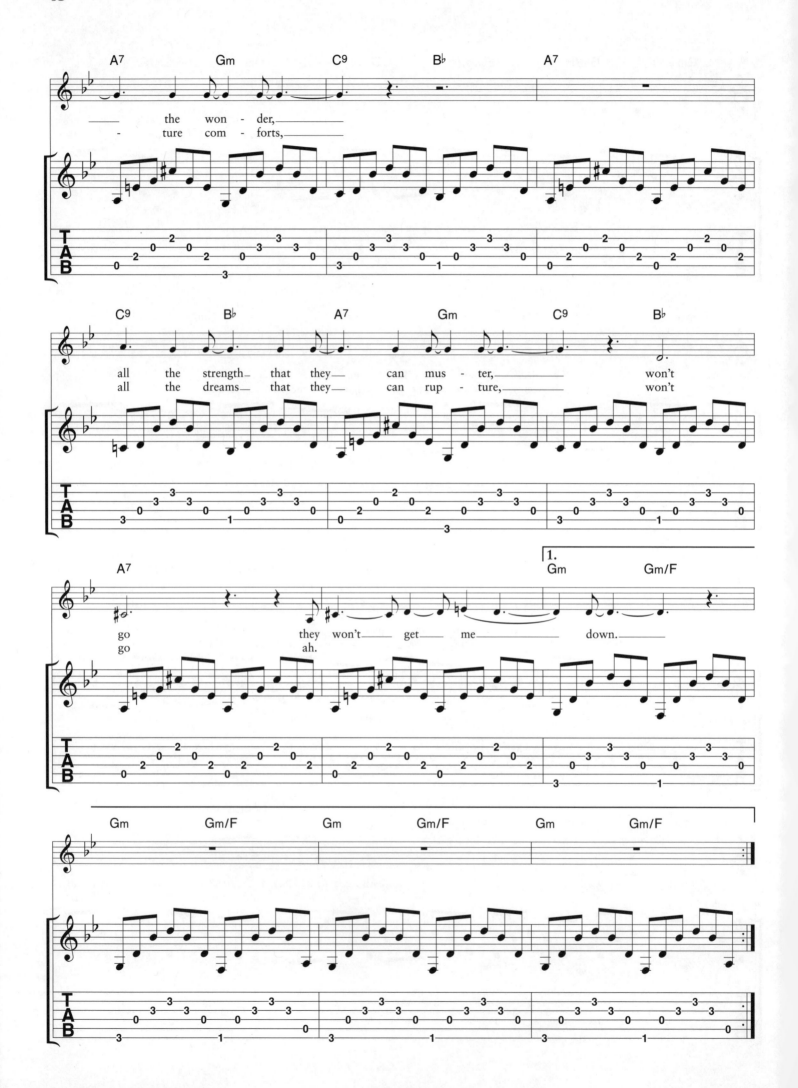

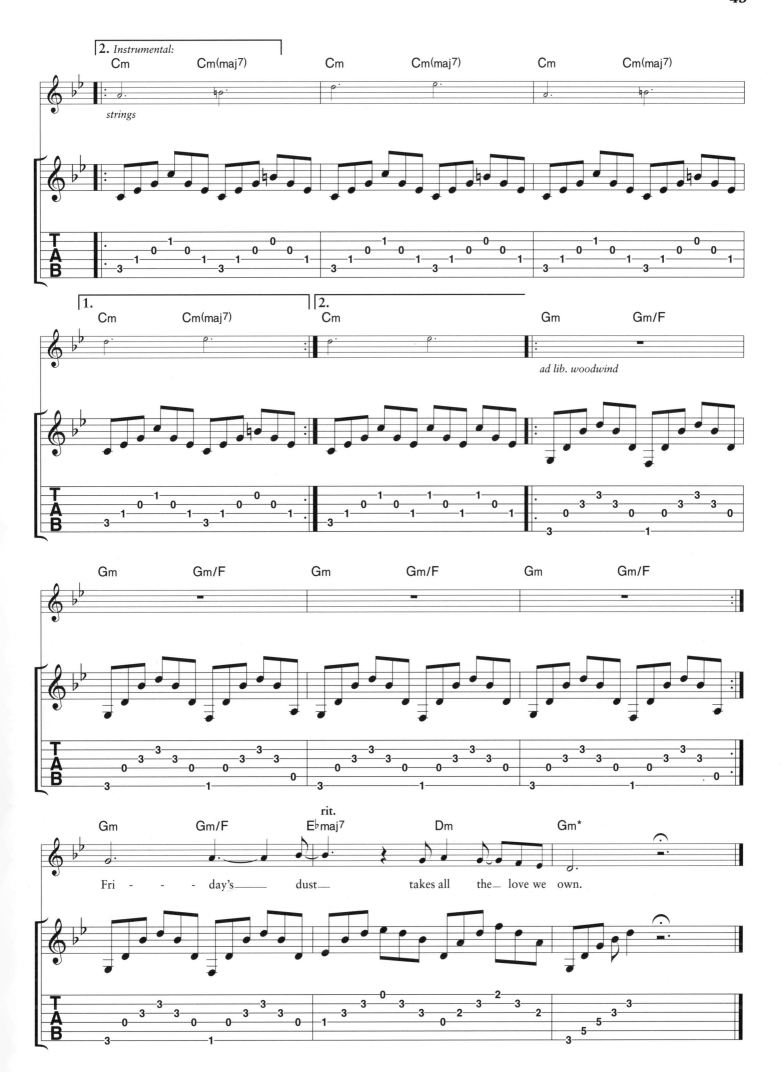

# SATELLITES

**Words and Music by Williams/Goodwin/Williams**

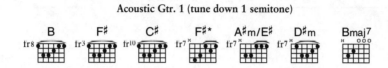

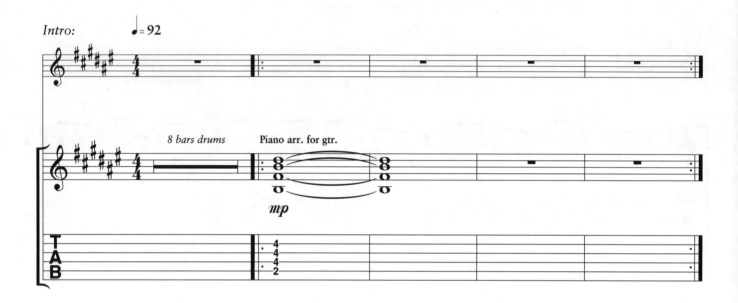

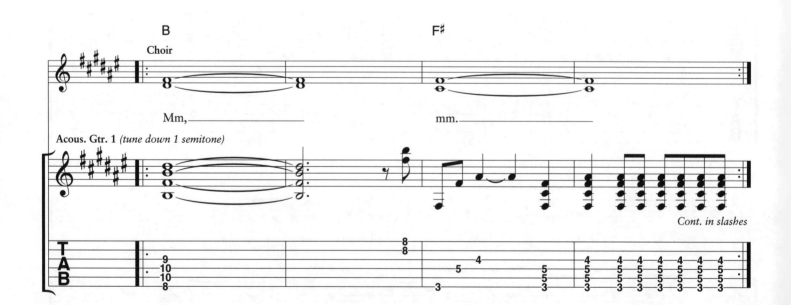

I want you to——know this,——
Here comes a strange car - go,——

my an - ger's all——but done.——— Sweet Lord,
here comes a light that leaves out of here. Sweet Lord,

I swear I've seen——the dark - ness. Sweet Lord,
and all I've known——is bad - ness. Sweet Lord,

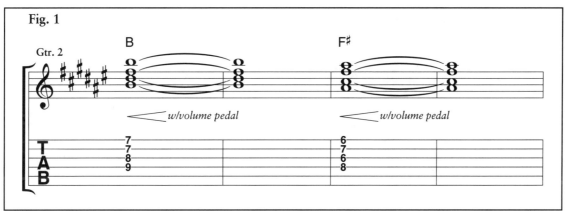

Fig. 1

I swear I've seen—— some pain.
and all I've known— is pain.

*1° w/Fig. 2 (Elec. Gtr. 2)*

**Chorus:**

*Cont. rhy. simile ad lib.*

Sat - el -lites a - head, so hold— on.—

*mf*

Sat - el -lites I———— said so come— on.—

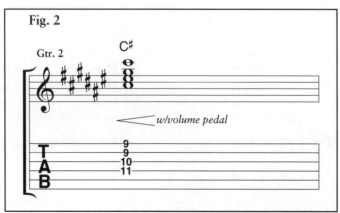

Fig. 2

Gtr. 2

*w/volume pedal*

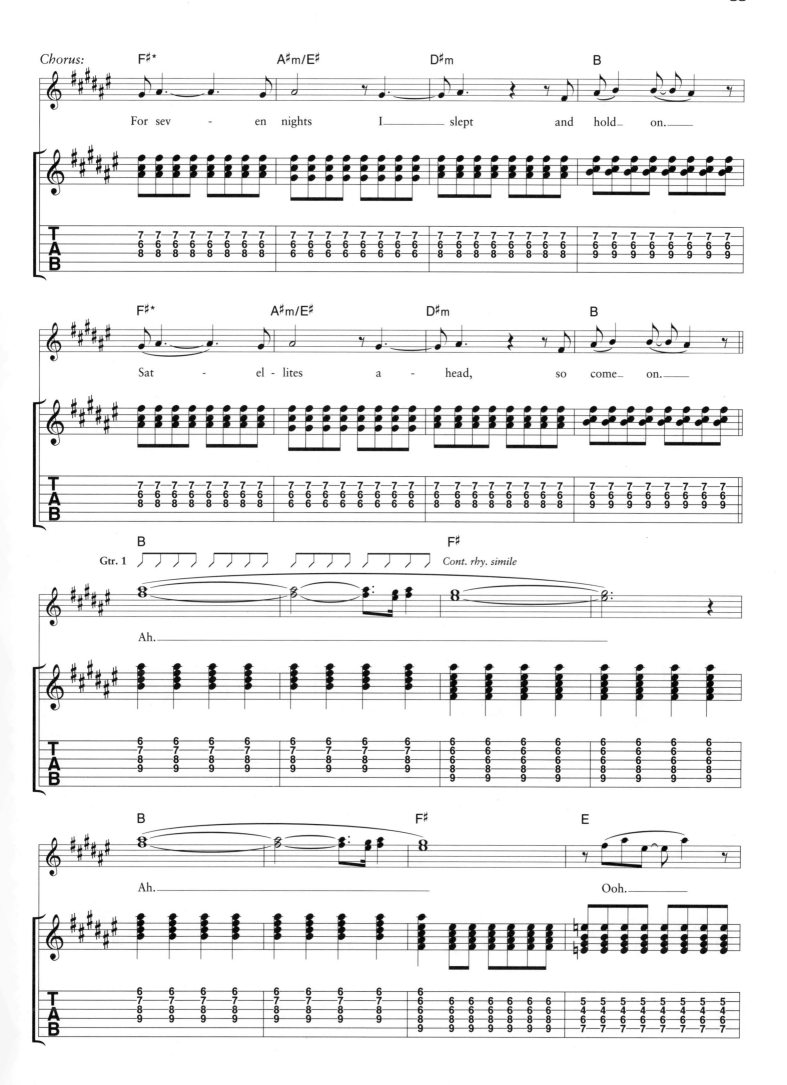

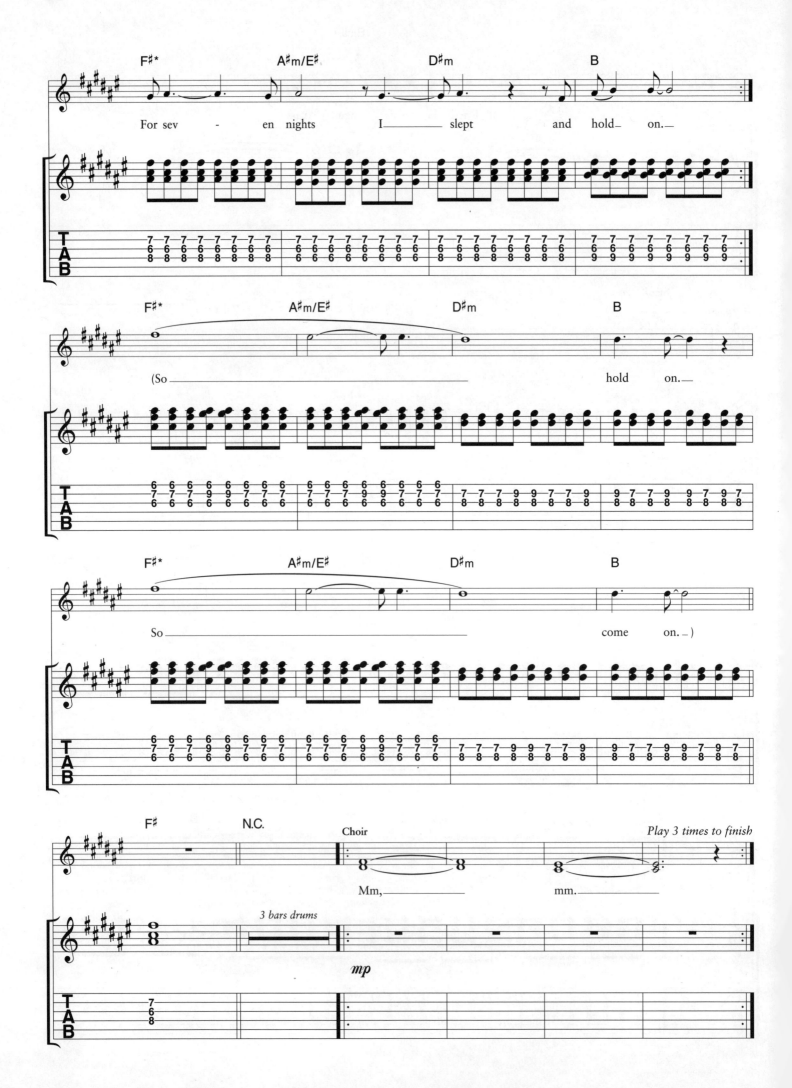

# POUNDING

**Words and Music by Williams/Goodwin/Williams**

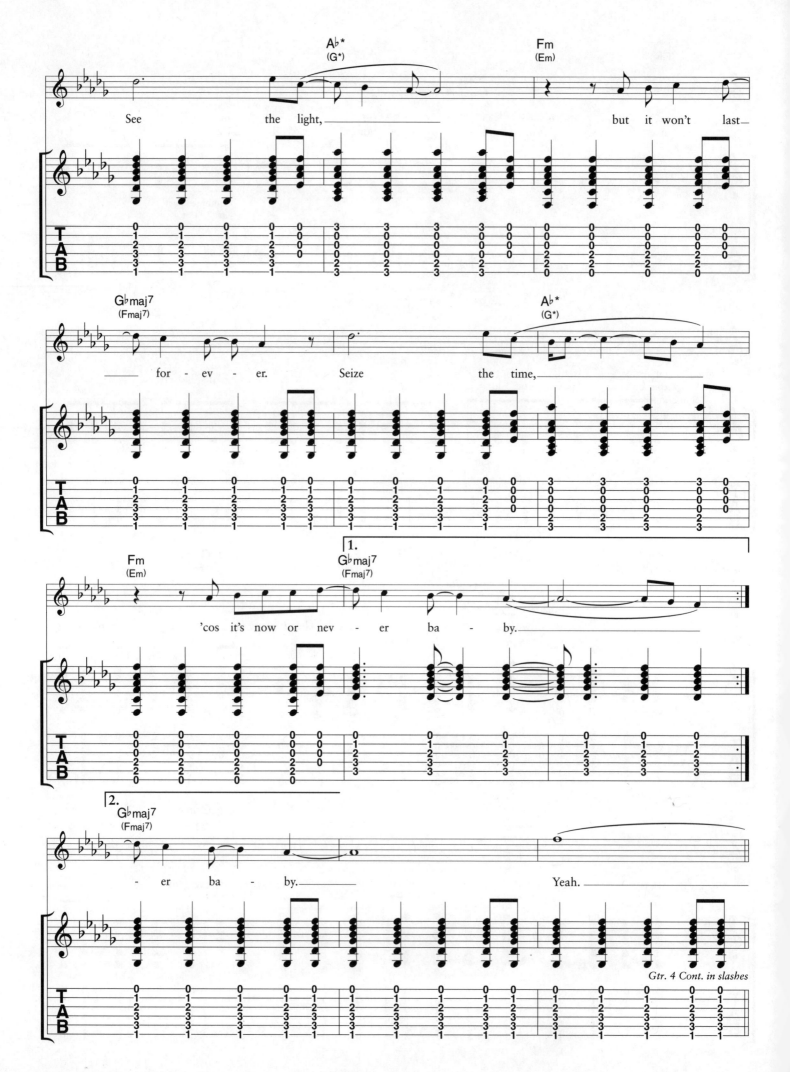

*Gtr. 4 Cont. in slashes*

# LAST BROADCAST

**Words and Music by Williams/Goodwin/Williams**

Yeah,_____ Gets to the point_ where you_ can't breathe,___ it's the
Ah,_____ it comes to a point_ when you feel no-thing. This is the

last_____ word,_____ and I can see you un-der - stand._____
last_____ time,_____ 'cos I can see it in your eyes._____

So here we are,_____ at the

2° w/Fig. 4 (Elec. Gtr. 3)

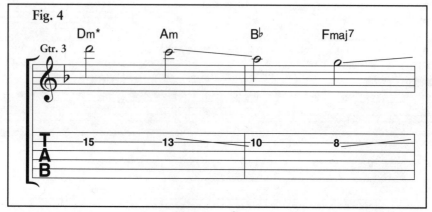

Fig. 4

Gtr. 3

last broad - - - cast._____ And here we are—

at the last broad - - - cast.

Elec. Gtr. 3

w/Fig. 1 *(Elec. Gtr. 1)*    *w/echo*

w/Fig. 2 *(Elec. Gtr. 4)*    Fig. 3...

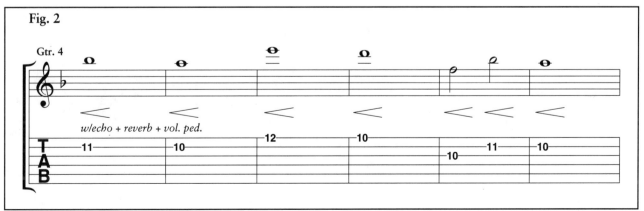

**Fig. 2**

Gtr. 4

*w/echo + reverb + vol. ped.*

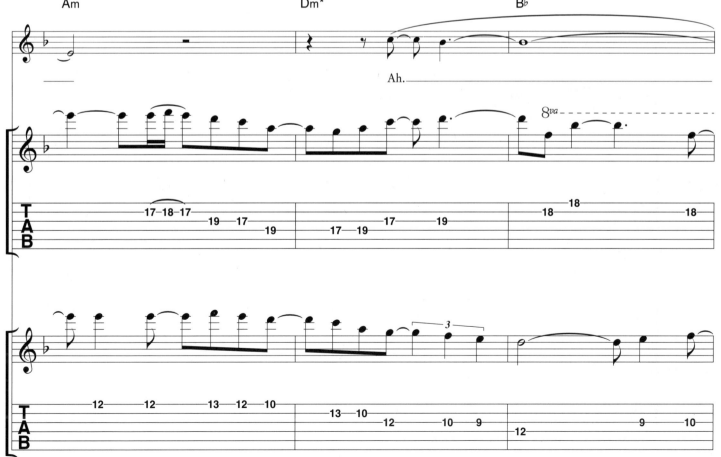

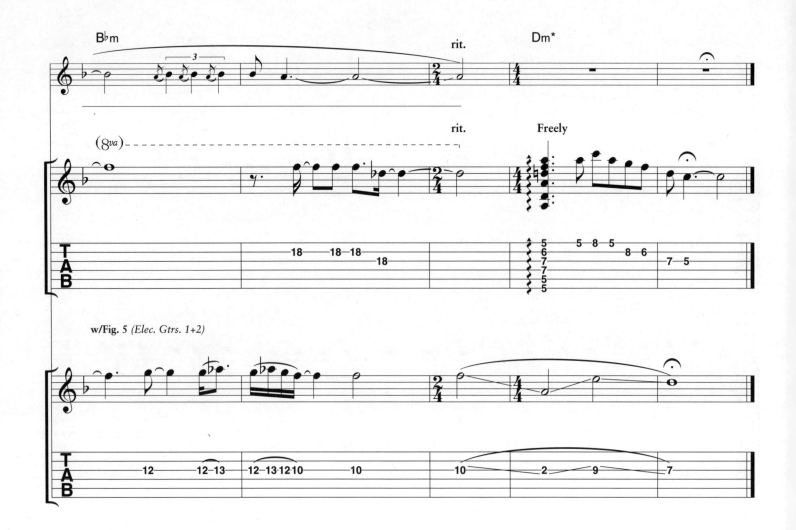

w/Fig. 5 (Elec. Gtrs. 1+2)

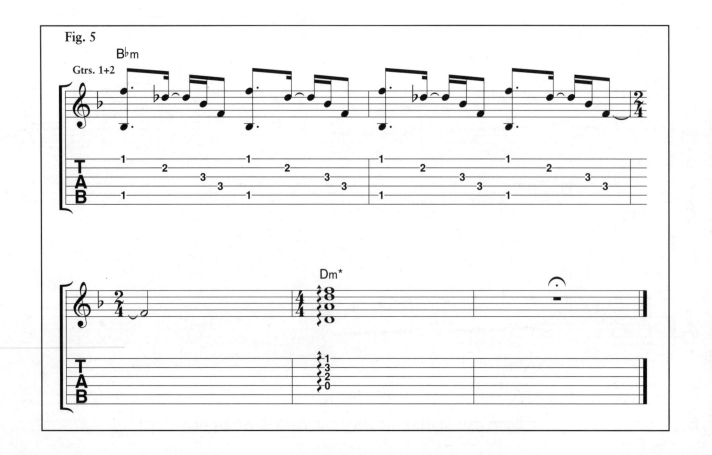

Fig. 5

# THE SULPHUR MAN

**Words and Music by Williams/Goodwin/Williams**

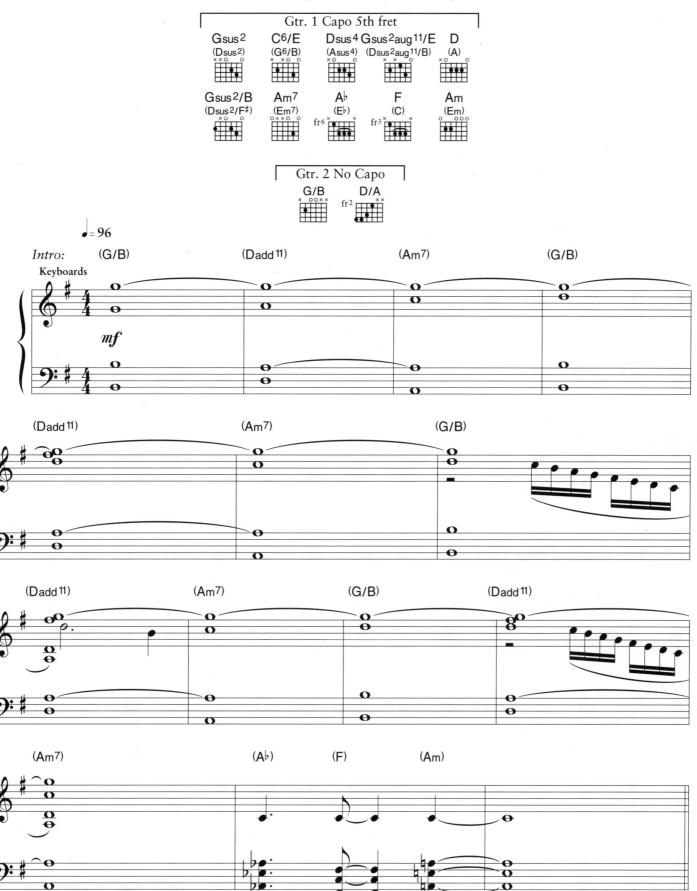

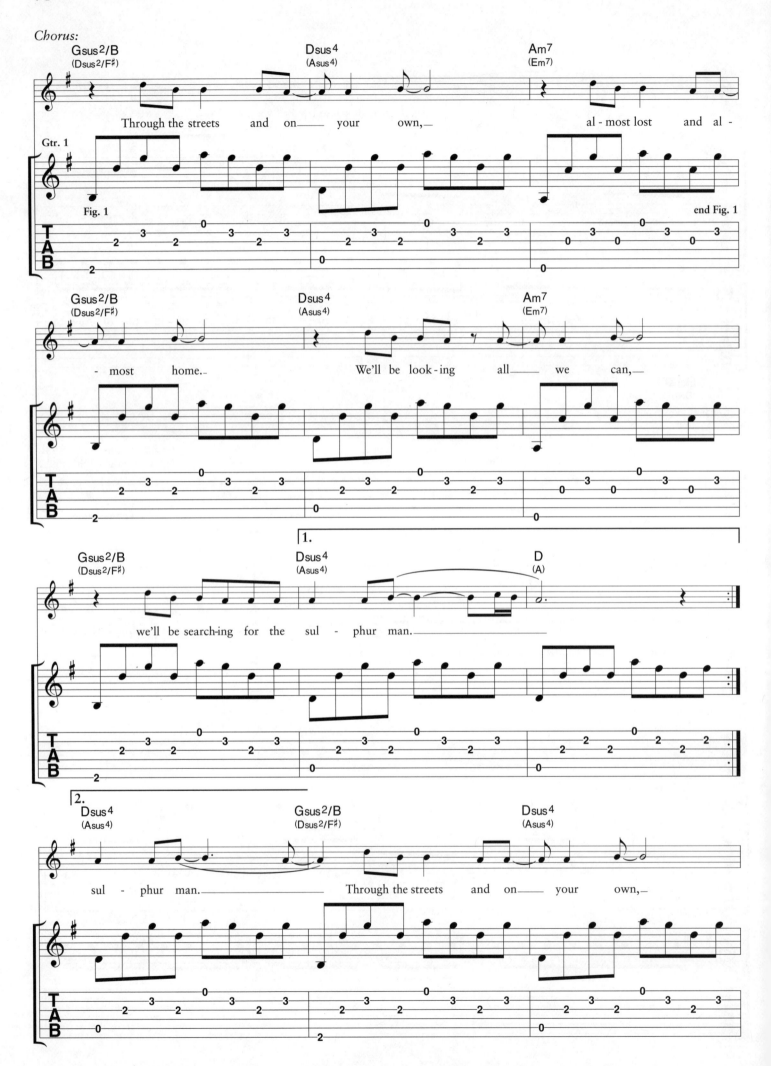

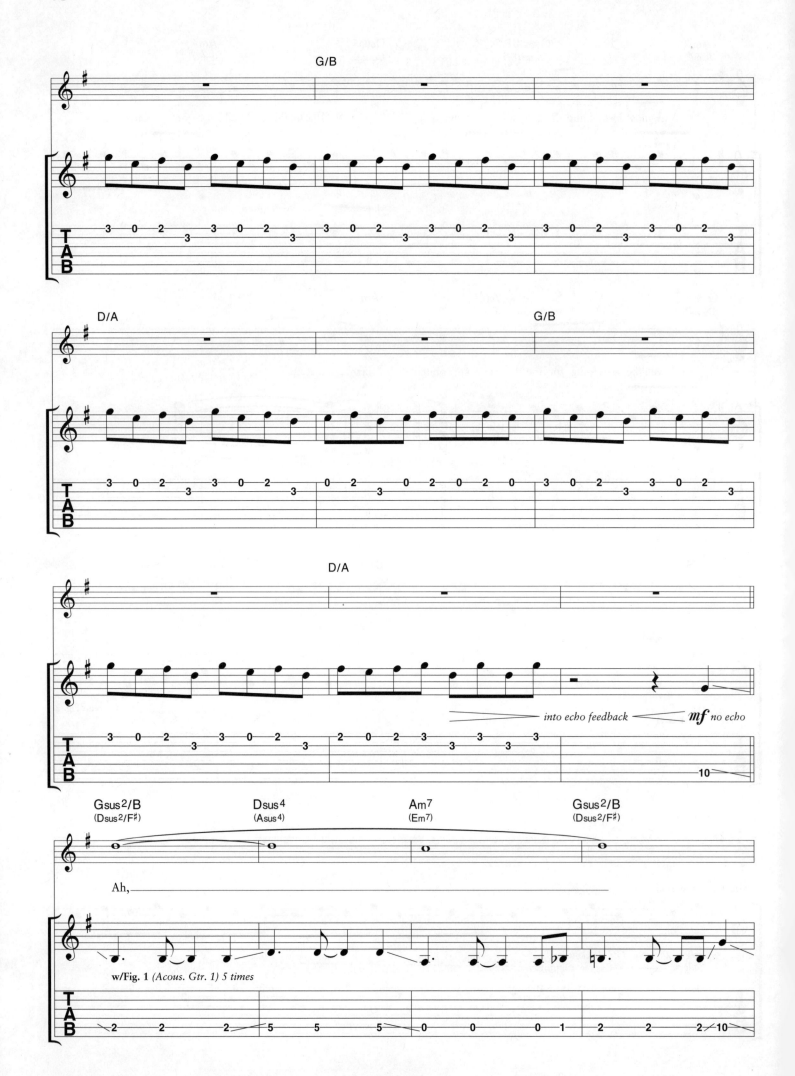

# CAUGHT BY THE RIVER

Words and Music by Williams/Goodwin/Williams

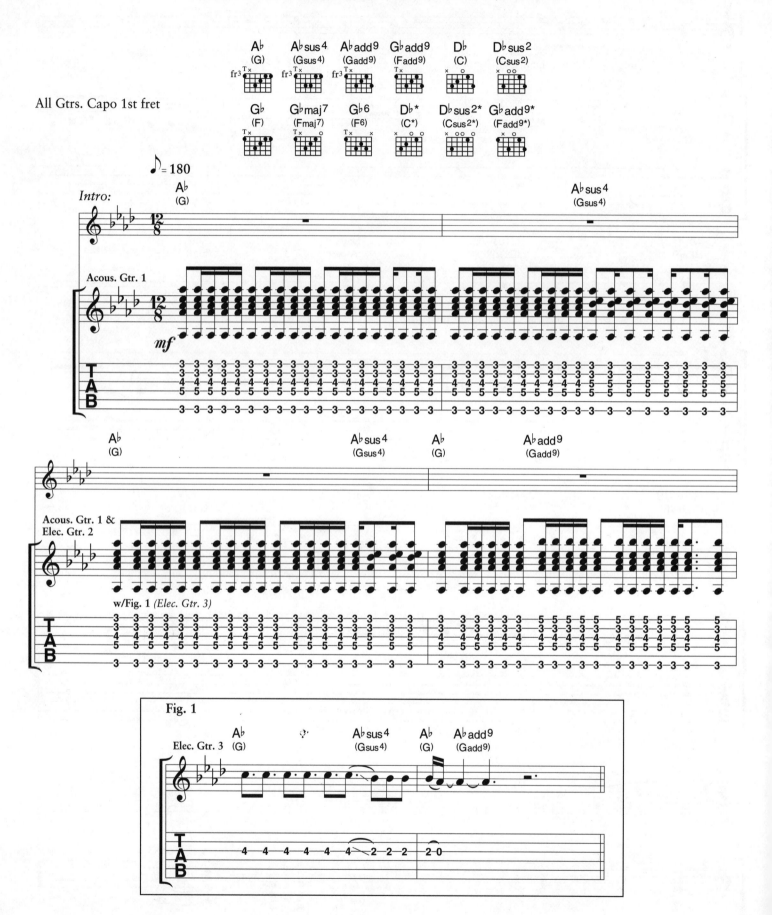

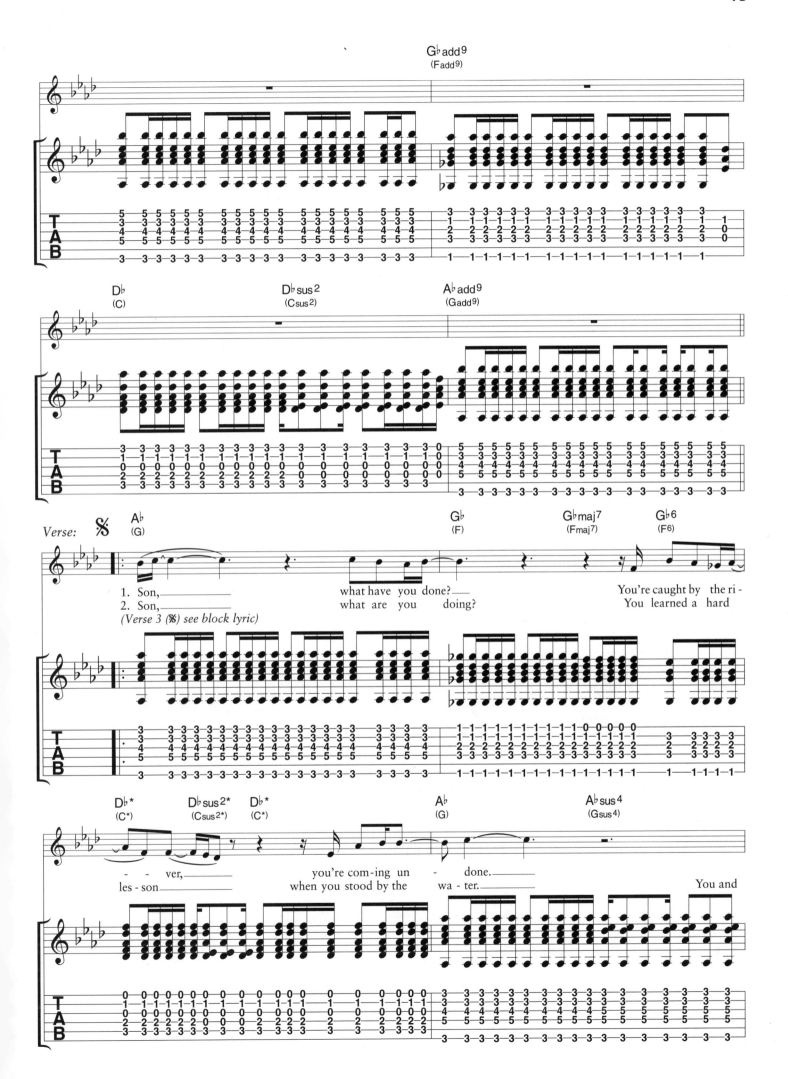

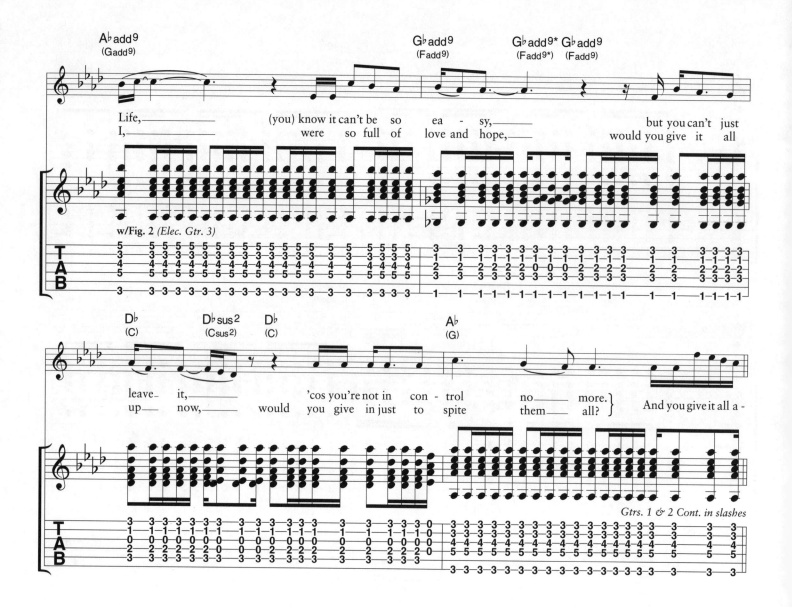

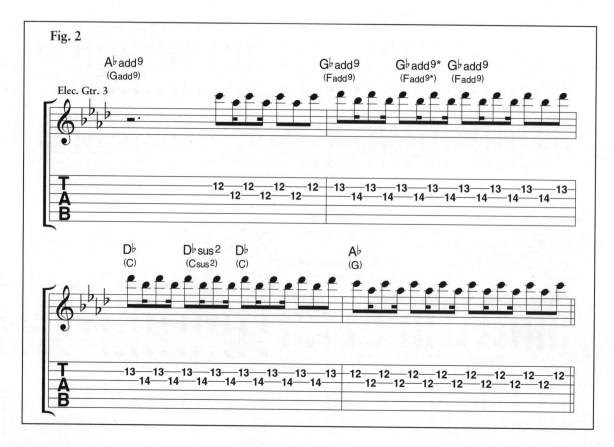

Fig. 2

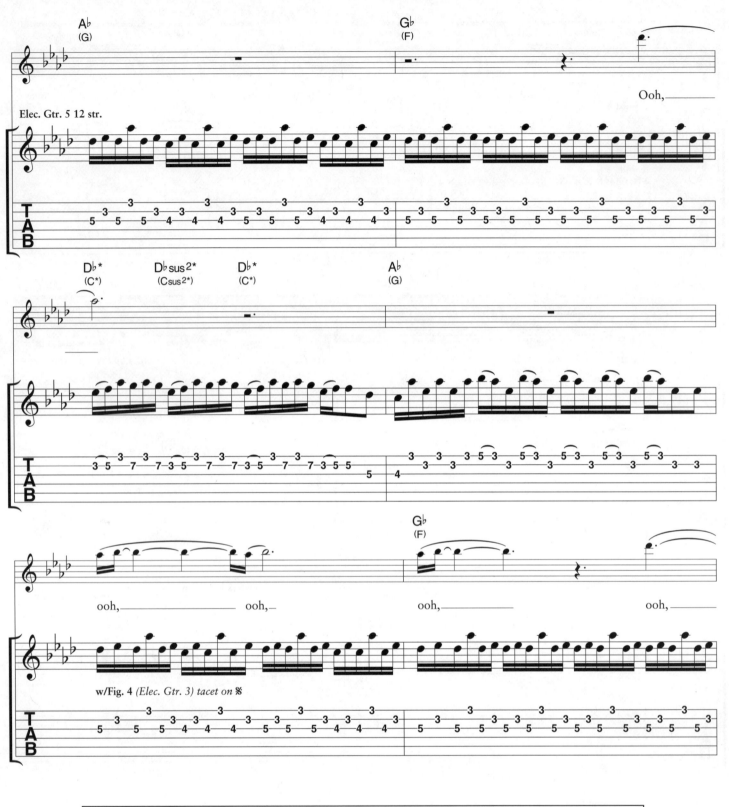

Ooh,————————

Elec. Gtr. 5 12 str.

ooh,——————— ooh,— ooh,— ooh,——

w/Fig. 4 (Elec. Gtr. 3) tacet on 𝄇

Fig. 4

Gtr. 3

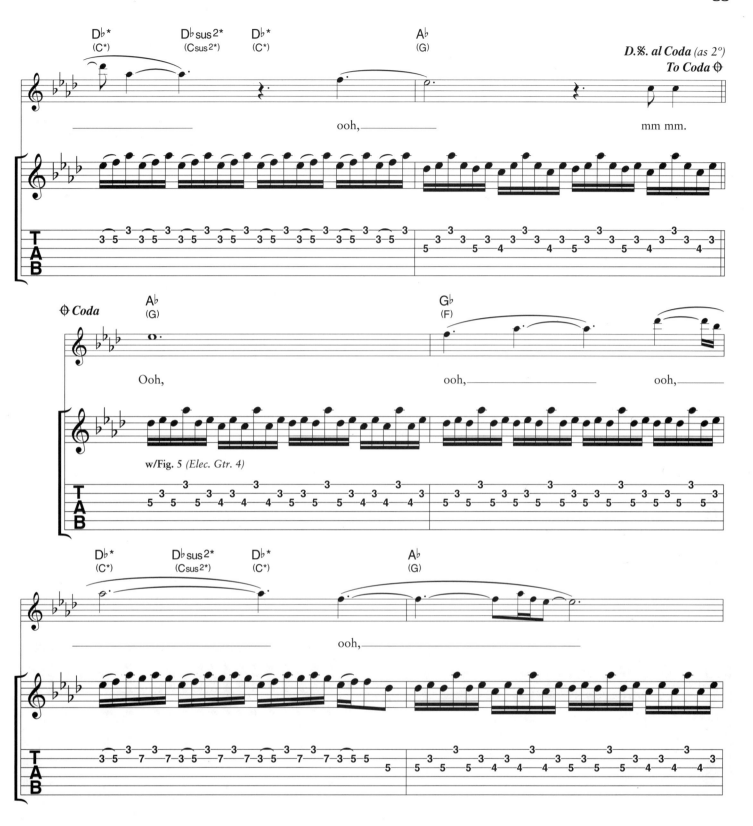

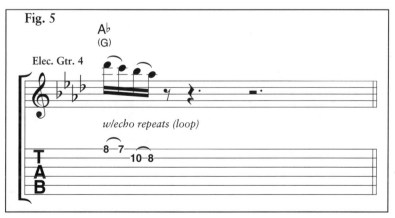

*2° fade out*

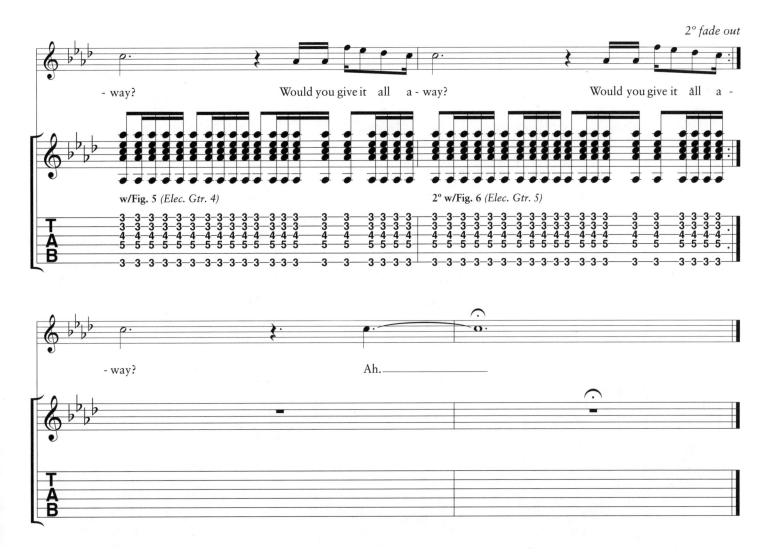

- way?  Would you give it all a - way?  Would you give it all a -

w/Fig. 5 *(Elec. Gtr. 4)*  2° w/Fig. 6 *(Elec. Gtr. 5)*

- way?  Ah.

Fig. 6

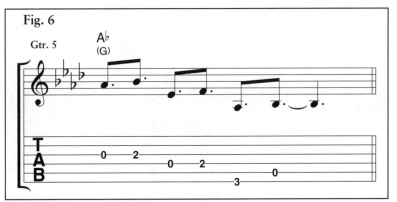

Gtr. 5

*Verse 3:*
Lay, I lay in the long grass
So many people
So many people pass
Ah stay, stay here and lie back
Down near the cornfields
Stay till we're caught at last.

GUITAR · TABLATURE · VOCAL

# doves
## lost souls

Also Available:
Doves Lost Souls

7471A          GTAB ISBN: 1-85909-922-X

Firesuite – Here It Comes – Break Me Gently – Sea Song – Rise – Lost Souls – Melody Calls –
Catch The Sun – The Man Who Told Everything – The Cedar Room – Reprise – A House

# Available Now

## In all good music shops

# ModernGuitar Anthems BlueBook

**Thirty songs arranged for Guitar Tablature Vocal.**

Starsailor/TheDandyWarhols/
Elbow/Feeder/TurinBrakes/
VexRed//TheElectricSoftParade/
TheWhiteStripes/Radiohead/
BlackRebelMotorcycleClub/
MercuryRev/Haven/TheCoral/
HundredReasons/A/TheMusic/
Doves/MullHistoricalSociety/
TheCooperTempleClause/Idlewild

International Music Publications Limited

MGAB